BASIC BOOK OF DAHLIA GROWING

IN THE SAME SERIES

Flower Gardening
Vegetable Growing
Rock Gardens and Pools
Chrysanthemum Growing
Rose Growing
Decorative Shrubs
Herbaceous Borders
Pruning Trees, Bushes and Shrubs

OTHER TITLES IN PREPARATION

BASIC BOOK OF DAHLIA GROWING

W. E. SHEWELL-COOPER
MBE, NDH, FLS, FRSL, Dip.Hort.(Wye), DLitt

BARRIE & JENKINS
COMMUNICA-EUROPA

First published 1976
by Barrie & Jenkins Ltd,
24 Highbury Crescent, London N5 1RX

ISBN 0 214 20135 X

Photoset, printed and bound
in Great Britain by
REDWOOD BURN LIMITED
Trowbridge & Esher

CONTENTS

		Page
	List of illustrations	6
	Preface	9
1	The history of the dahlia	11
2	The classification of dahlias	15
3	Dahlia propagation	21
4	Preparing and feeding the soil	44
5	Planting dahlias	56
6	Managing dahlias	65
7	Dahlias as cut flowers	77
8	Dahlias in the greenhouse	84
9	Dahlias as bedding plants	91
10	Showing dahlias	98
11	Cactus and Semi-Cactus Dahlias	109
12	Decorative Dahlias	115
13	Pompon Dahlias	125
14	Ball Dahlias	127
15	Miscellaneous dahlias	129
16	Pests and diseases	134
17	What to do month by month	153
	Appendix	158
	Index	169

List of Illustrations

Black and white photographs and line drawings

	Page
'Mohair'	20
'Eyes' appearing at the base of an old tuber stem	26
A divided tuber root	26
Cutting with a small wedge-shaped piece of the parent tuber	27
Cutting and tuber being secured with raffia	28
Digging up well-established roots with a spade	29
Dry roots being trimmed ready for storing	30
A tuber ready for storage	31
Peat and coarse sand for rooting dahlia cuttings	32
Making a cutting	35
Cutting ready for insertion. Cuttings in a pot	35
Watering dahlias	67
Setting canes to support your dahlias	71
Methods of tying up using flexible wire	72
String framework for supporting a plant	72
How to cut flowers, so as to have a continuous display	74
Disbudding a dahlia	75
'Twiggy'	80
Using an insecticide in the greenhouse	90
Staging exhibition dahlias	103
Decorative Dahlias	117
Small-flowered Pompon Dahlias	125
Collarette Dahlias	129
Anemone-flowered Dahlias	130
Paeony-flowered Dahlias	131
Single Dahlias	132
Using a pressure sprayer	136
Upturned pots filled with straw for trapping earwigs	143
The pH scale	161

Colour plates

Colour plates	*Facing page*
Dwarf bedding dahlia, 'Red Flash'	48
'Crystello'	49
'De Sarasate'	64
'Jimmy Meredith'	65
'Holland Festival'	112
'Purple Globe'	113
'Fascination', a Paeony-flowered variety	128
'Sincerity', a Collarette variety	129

Acknowledgements
The author would like to thank Mr R. H. M. Robinson, of the Harry Smith Horticultural Photographic Collection, for kindly supplying the colour photographs facing pages 48, 112, 113, 128 and 129 and Philip Damp for supplying those facing pages 49, 64 and 65.

To David R. Shillitoe
who has helped regularly at the open days
of the Good Gardeners' Association

Preface

I have been growing dahlias now for over forty years. I started in quite a small way with the bedding types and then graduated to the taller varieties, growing some for show, some in the mixed flower border and others as cut flowers.

In my book *Modern Flower Growing for Profit*, first published by Messrs Ernest Benn in 1933, lists were given of dahlias which could be grown successfully for florist shops. Then special dahlia trials were carried out at The Cheshire Agricultural College when I was Horticultural Superintendent there, and these were continued when I moved down to Kent as Superintendent of the Swanley Horticultural College.

With the assistance of Mrs Barbara Argles (née Wates), experiments were carried out on the keeping qualities of dahlias. Then came trials concerned with manuring, mulching and staking, and when we moved the International Horticultural Advisory Bureau to Thaxted in 1950, we gave demonstrations on the growing of dahlias under glass, with which we had some extremely encouraging results.

It was my privilege, for a number of years, to live in the village in which Stuart Ogg's nursery was situated. The owner, 'Teddy' Ogg, used to come to my home, and I, of course, could go to his nursery at any time to 'talk dahlias'. At that time I took a particular interest in his work; no one had won more large Gold Medals for dahlias than he. I would like to thank Teddy Ogg for his kind co-operation in the preparation of the original version of this book, *Guide to Dahlias*. (This became *The A.B.C. of Dahlias*, which in its turn has been expanded and revised, for this new series of Basic Books of Gardening.)

I should also like to thank Mrs Gweneth Johnson, Dip.Hort. (Swanley) for her help. Miss J. P. Russell, Gold Medallist RHS, read the original proofs and made suggestions, and she is of course thanked also. I should like to thank Mrs Gordon for typing the script so patiently.

My special thanks are due to Mr Philip Damp, General Secretary of the National Dahlia Society, for all his help in dotting the 'i's and crossing the 't's, and in providing really up-to-date lists of varieties.

Arkley Manor,
Arkley,
South Herts.

W. E. SHEWELL-COOPER
July 1975

1 The History of the Dahlia

I have in my library a wonderful old book, *The Gardeners' Dictionary*, written by Philip Miller, FRS, who was Gardener to the Worshipful Company of Apothecaries at their Botanic Garden in Chelsea. It was published in 1863 and though I searched and searched in this lovely old volume I could find no mention at all of the dahlia, though there is much about the 'Delphinium', the 'Datura', the 'Doronicum' and the 'Digitalis'. Another book, however, the *Royal Encyclopaedia* written by the Rev. J. M. Wilson in 1853, does mention the dahlia as a genus of tuberous-rooted, magnificently flowering, Mexican plants belonging to the sunflower division of the *Compositae* order.

The dahlia, of course, was named in honour of Dr Andreas Dahl, the famous Swedish botanist who was a pupil of Linnaeus, after whom the Linnaean Society was named. It belongs to the family *Compositae* and consists of a genus of a dozen species of Mexican herbaceous plants. The roots are always tuberous, the stems are branching, the leaves are opposite, and the flower heads are invariably long-stalked. Very few of the actual species are grown today and most of the varieties mentioned in this book come from hybrids between the species or as variations which have arisen during past cultivations.

The true varieties cannot be reproduced perfectly from seed. They have to be propagated vegetatively. That is to say, cuttings must be taken or the tuberous roots must be split up. The official horicultural classification, as approved by the Royal Horticultural Society and the National Dahlia Society, will be found set out in Chapter 2.

Some horticultural historians have suggested that the dahlia was introduced into this country by the Marchioness of Bute in 1789 and came to this country via Spain. It became lost because of ignorance of its culture and so had to be reintroduced into Great Britain in 1804. The fact is that the dahlia came from Mexico to the Botanic Gardens in Madrid in 1789. From Spain the dahlia passed to France and it was not until 1802 that it arrived in this country and flowered at Chelsea in 1803. The particular species appears to have been *Dahlia coccinea*. The species *Dahlia rosea* is also reported to have flowered at Vauxhall in 1803.

There is little doubt that the Marchioness of Bute did send three species of dahlias from Madrid to the Royal Botanic Gardens at Kew in 1789, but these unfortunately were lost. Lady Holland also sent some seed home from Madrid in 1804. Another keen gardener, it is reported, brought a quite different stock of dahlias from France in 1815. These were propagated from seed with the result that a large number of different garden varieties were produced. Since that time hundreds of varieties have been raised in various parts of Europe and the United States of America, and these are described later on in the various chapters.

Originally, the dahlia was described botanically as the georgina. The fertile-rayed species, *Georgina pinnata*, was eventually named *Dahlia superflua*, while the barren-rayed species, *Georgina frustranea*, which was the one introduced in 1802, was renamed *Dahlia frustranea*. Incidentally, in most countries of the world 'dahlia' is pronounced with a short 'a', as in 'ah', whereas in this country it is invariably pronounced with a long 'a', as in 'day'.

It can perhaps be said that *Dahlia variabilis* is the parent of the majority of the present forms of this very variable plant. In its original form it was a yellow disc-like 'symbol', having a very light row of dull red rays, but during the nineteenth century the breeders got hold of it and a great range of brightly coloured, fully double flowers was produced. My ancient Encyclopaedia tells me that 'the astonishing and ever active prolificity with which all seeding dahlias produce new varieties renders minute classification undesirable.' It goes on to say: 'It rushed into popularity with the speed of lightning; it enraptured all sorts of florists in a great degree to the neglect of former favourites; it seized on the minds of myriads and worked in them almost in the manner of a mania; but although confessively a most gorgeous plant, it has become so universally diffused as to have fairly receded fellowship with the aristocratic beauties of the flower garden, and to be already of little more consideration than the common but superb hollyhock.' The National Dahlia Society, I feel, will hardly agree with these remarks.

History also relates that the tubers were tried as a vegetable, in Paris in the early 1800s, and for fifteen years, at about that period, they were sold in the city markets of Britain under the assumed name of Jerusalem Artichokes. Evidently they were grown and stored in a similar manner to potatoes, though originally disliked by both man and beast. They were found to be rich in nutritive matter, and one author of an old agricultural textbook states that 'with the slight aid from chemistry the dahlia may be rendered well worthy of field culture and farmyard consumption.' I can find no trace, however, that the dahlia was ever grown in tens of acres by farmers, either to feed the cattle or to sell as a market garden crop.

In the evolution of the modern dahlia there has naturally been a tremendous amount of crossing and intercrossing. *Dahlia groccinea* is said to be the progenitor of all the singles and all their variations. In the nineteenth century, *Dahlia juarezii* was introduced and has proved to be the parent of the Cactus varieties.

I am very fascinated by the story of Abbé Cavanilles, who was Horticultural Superintendent of the Royal Gardens in Madrid in the late 1700s. He wrote a book called *Icones* and described in it this new plant of which he evidently had three varieties, *Dahlia pinnata*, *Dahlia rosea* and *Dahlia coccinea*. These three were the only parents of the garden and show varieties we have today – until the introduction of the Cactus-flowered.

There is no doubt that our forebears did a great deal of work on the dahlia, and from single flower types produced the lovely doubles which we have today. It was not long before specialist Dahlia Societies were formed, and Shows were held all over the country. There are records that from 1820 to 1860 Shows were held in hundreds of towns and villages. Fancy and Show Dahlias figured largely in these. It was in 1829 that the Anemone-flowered Dahlia first appeared, and in 1850 the Pompons, which came to us from Germany. These were originally known as Bouquet or Lilliputian Dahlias and they became 'all the rage'.

The National Dahlia Society was founded in 1870. The next event was the introduction of the first Cactus Dahlia by Henry Cannell of Swanley Junction in 1879. He produced a brilliant scarlet dahlia of this type. Then came the introduction of Singles in 1880, said to be raised by Mr E. W. Lowe of Chepstow, and from that time onwards, for twenty years or more, hundreds of different Cactus types were produced. It is a pity, however, that the raisers in those days paid little attention to dahlias as a garden plant, and so most of the flowers produced had very weak stems and hung their heads. They were grand for exhibiting on show boards but useless in the garden. Furthermore, the foliage was so strong that the flowers were largely hidden.

It was Mr George Gordon, President of the National Dahlia Society, who, with his facile pen, begged raisers to pay more attention to the dahlia as a garden flower. His lead was followed by Mr Reginald Cory, who had the vision of carrying out the first trial of dahlias at Duffryn near Cardiff, under the auspices of the National Dahlia Society and the Royal Horticultural Society. It is said that at that first trial held in 1913, over 8,000 plants were included. This 'made' the dahlia from the point of view of the general public. Today it is one of the most popular flowers grown.

In 1922 the dwarf Coltness Gem types of dahlias were first introduced. This actually started quite a new race of bedding varieties which is very popular today, so much so that the whole of Chapter 8 is devoted to these plants. Originally all bedding varieties were single, but now there are almost as many doubles.

I would advise all keen dahlia growers to join the National Dahlia Society. Write to Mr Philip Damp, General Secretary of the National Dahlia Society, 26 Burns Road, Leamington Spa, Warwickshire, mentioning this book, and I am sure he will be very pleased to welcome you as a member.

2 The Classification of Dahlias

The following revised classification and description of dahlias has been published by the National Dahlia Society in their handbook, to assist exhibitors in making entries in particular classes. I am glad to have the privilege of quoting much of the relevant material.

This classification was brought up to date in 1966 through the joint efforts of the National Dahlia Society and the Royal Horticultural Society's Committee.

Abbreviations

Group Classification and Formation

Group		
I	Single	Sin.
II	Anemone-flowered	Anem.
III	Collarette	Col.
IV	Paeony-flowered	Pae.
V(A)	Decorative, giant	G.D.
V(B)	Decorative, large	L.D.
V(C)	Decorative, medium	M.D.
V(D)	Decorative, small	S.D.
V(E)	Decorative, miniature	Min.D.
VI(A)	Small Ball	Ba.
VI(B)	Miniature Ball	Min.Ba.
VII	Pompon	Pom.
VIII(A)	Cactus, giant	G.C.
VIII(B)	Cactus, large	L.C.
VIII(C)	Cactus, medium	M.C.
VIII(D)	Cactus, small	S.C.
VIII(E)	Cactus, miniature	Min.C.
IX(A)	Semi-Cactus, giant	G.S.C.
IX(B)	Semi-Cactus, large	L.S.C.
IX(C)	Semi-Cactus, medium	M.S.C.
IX(D)	Semi-Cactus, small	S.S.C.
IX(E)	Semi-Cactus, miniature	Min.S.C.
X	Miscellaneous, inc.	Misc.
	Orchid-flowering	Orc.
	Botanical	Bot.
—	Dwarf Bedding	Dw.B.
—	Fimbriated	Fim.

Group I Single-flowered Dahlias have blooms with a single outer ring of florets, which may overlap, the centre forming a disc.

Group II Anemone-flowered Dahlias have blooms with one or more outer rings of generally flattened ray florets surrounding a dense group of tubular florets (which are longer than the disc florets in single dahlias), and showing no disc. (The small letters under 'colour' indicate the colouration of the cushion.)

Group III Collarette Dahlias have blooms with a single outer ring of generally flat ray florets. These may overlay the central disc with a ring of small florets, forming a 'collar'. (The small letters under 'colour' indicate the colouration of the collar.)

Group IV Paeony-flowered Dahlias have blooms with two or more rings of generally flattened ray florets, the centre forming a disc.

Group V Decorative Dahlias have fully double blooms showing no disc. The ray florets are broad, scarcely revolute or involute along their length (longitudinal axis), generally flat or slightly twisted and usually bluntly pointed.

Group V (A) Giant-flowered Decorative Dahlias have blooms usually over 254 mm (10 in.) in diameter.

Group V (B) Large-flowered Decorative Dahlias have blooms usually between 203 mm (8 in.) and 254 mm (10 in.) in diameter.

Group V (C) Medium-flowered Decorative Dahlias have blooms usually between 152 mm (6 in.) and 203 mm (8 in.) in diameter.

Group V (D) Small-flowered Decorative Dahlias have blooms usually between 102 mm (4 in.) and 152 mm (6 in.) in diameter.

Group V (E) Miniature-flowered Decorative Dahlias have blooms not usually exceeding 102 mm (4 in.) in diameter.

Group VI Ball Dahlias have fully double blooms, ball shaped or slightly flattened. The ray florets blunt or rounded at the tips, with margins spirally arranged and involute for more than half the length of the florets.

Group VI (A) Small Ball Dahlias have blooms usually between 102 mm (4 in.) and 152 mm (6 in.) in diameter.

Group VI (B) Miniature Ball Dahlias have blooms not usually exceeding 102 mm (4 in.) in diameter.

(*Please note*: Section VI (A), previously *Ball Dahlias*, is now *Small Ball.*)

Group VII Pompon Dahlias have blooms similar to those of Ball Dahlias, but more globular and of miniature size (not exceeding 51 mm (2 in.) in diameter for exhibition), with florets involute for the whole of their length (longitudinal axis).

Group VIII Cactus Dahlias have fully double blooms. The ray florets are usually pointed, the majority narrow and revolute for more than half their length (longitudinal axis), and either straight or incurving.

Group VIII (A) Giant-flowered Cactus Dahlias have blooms usually over 254 mm (10 in.) in diameter.

Group VIII (B) Large-flowered Cactus Dahlias have blooms usually between 203 mm (6 in.) and 254 mm (10 in.) in diameter.

Group VIII (C) Medium-flowered Cactus Dahlias have blooms usually between 152 mm (6 in.) and 203 mm (8 in.) in diameter.

Group VIII (D) Small-flowered Cactus Dahlias have blooms usually between 102 mm (4 in.) and 152 mm (6 in.) in diameter.

Group VIII (E) Miniature-flowered Cactus Dahlias have blooms not usually exceeding 102 mm (4 in.) in diameter.

Group IX Semi-Cactus Dahlias have fully double blooms. The ray florets are usually pointed, the majority narrower than those of Decorative Dahlias, but broader than those of Cactus Dahlias, and revolute for half their length (longitudinal axis) or less, broad at the base, and either straight or incurving.

Group IX (A) Giant-flowered Semi-Cactus Dahlias have blooms usually 254 mm (10 in.) in diameter.

Group IX (B) Large-flowered Semi-Cactus Dahlias have blooms usually between 203 mm (8 in.) and 254 mm (10 in.) in diameter.

Group IX (C) Medium-flowered Semi-Cactus Dahlias have blooms usually between 152 mm (6 in.) and 203 mm (8 in.) in diameter.

Group IX (D) Small-flowered Semi-Cactus Dahlias have blooms usually between 102 mm (4 in.) and 152 mm (6 in.) in diameter.

Group IX (E) Miniature-flowered Semi-Cactus Dahlias have blooms not usually exceeding 102 mm (4 in.) in diameter.

Group X Miscellaneous Dahlias Any dahlias which do not fall into one of the foregoing groups, e.g. Orchid-flowering Dahlias, are included under this heading. (The blooms of Orchid-flowering dahlias are similar to those of Single Dahlias, except that the rays are involute, with the margins meeting or overlapping for at least two-thirds of their length, from the tip towards the base.)

The abbreviation 'Fim.', after the name and classification of a cultivar, indicates a fimbriated type, and the abbreviation 'Dw.B.', after the name and classification of a cultivar, indicates that these are plants of dwarf bedding dahlias which do not usually exceed 609 mm (24 in.) in height.

Colour Classification

For the purpose of colour classification, all colours, shades, tints, hues and combinations thereof found in the cultivated forms of the dahlia have been grouped in the thirteen divisions given below.

Colour classification is determined by the predominant colour or colours which appear on the face of the ray florets, and in such classification the colour of the reverse of the ray florets is not generally taken into consideration. An exception is made in the case of certain Orchid-flowered, Pompon or Ball Dahlias.

Cultivars classified in colour must not be exhibited in any other colour class other than that indicated in the alphabetical list of cultivars.

Cultivars not included in this list may be shown in groups appropriate to their colour.

In the case of blended, bicoloured or variegated cultivars the first colour indicated is the dominant colour, and such cultivars may be exhibited in classes for blooms of their dominant colour except where separate classes for blended and/or bicoloured and/or variegated cultivars are included in the show schedule.

White Includes pale cream, ivory and colours that are nearly white or cream.

Yellow All shades of yellow including Dresden, primrose, sulphur, mimosa, straw, lemon, amber yellow, chrome yellow (light) and maize.

Orange All shades of orange including saffron, cadmium, apricot, tangerine and Indian orange.

Flame Includes spectral blends, xanthic in origin, of scarlet red or orange with yellow including Saturn red, Mars orange, nasturtium, fire red and poppy red.

Bronze Includes buff, yellow ochre, majolica yellow, Spanish orange, ochraceous orange, tan, zinc orange, terracotta, burnt orange, cinnamon and greyed suffusions and blends of such tones with pink and lavender.

Red Includes all shades of red from mandarin red to scarlet and crimson, and also cherry, claret rose, currant red, vermilion and carmine.

Dark Red Includes cardinal, ox blood, chrysanthemum crimson.

Light Pink Includes pale tints of orange-red and scarlets including salmon, peach, orient pink, shell pink, azalea pink, coral pink, Venetian pink, French rose, porcelain rose, Delft rose and empire rose.

Dark Pink Includes tints and pinks of bluish tones including carmine rose, camellia rose, dawn pink, neyron rose, tyrian rose pink, china rose, phlox pink, spinel pink, rose pink, rhodamine pink, fuchsine pink.

Lilac, Lavender or Mauve Includes all light tints of magenta, purple and violet and to include mauve, heliotrope, lilac and lavender.

Purple, Wine and Violet Includes solferino purple, Indian lake, magenta, magenta rose, ruby red, garnet lake, purple madder, peony purple, dianthus purple, beetroot purple, maroon, petunia purple, imperial purple, royal purple, amethyst violet and violet.

Blends Cultivars in which two or more colours intermingel and gradually merge into each other.

Bicoloured and Variegated Cultivars in which the ground colour is tipped, striped or splashed with another colour.

Abbreviations

White	W	Light Pink	Lt Pk
Yellow	Y	Dark Pink	Dk Pk
Orange	O	Lilac, Lavender or Mauve	L
Bronze	B	Wine, Purple and Violets	Pu
Flame	Fl	Blends	Bls
Red	R	Bicoloured	Bic
Dark Red	Dk R	Variegated	Var

The ruby-red bicoloured dahlia 'Mohair', with white tips

3 Dahlia Propagation

There are four ways of propagating dahlias: (1) seed sowing, (2) division of tubers, (3) grafting and (4) taking cuttings. The last method is the simplest and most usual one, and it does, of course, ensure that plants come up true to name and true to colour. Gardeners have told me that seed sowing is the most interesting and exciting method because, as they point out, 'you never know what you're going to get'. Strong healthy plants are produced from seed, and this is an important point in these days when virulent virus diseases are decimating the stock of many varieties today. You cannot guarantee, however, obtaining plants true to type and colour in every case, for the dahlia does not reproduce itself perfectly from seed.

It has been shown by raisers that the garden forms, as well as the species of dahlias, are what is termed 'self-sterile'. This means that seed is not produced if the female pistil of the flower is pollinated by pollen from its own stamens. Therefore, as cross-fertilization is necessary in order to ensure seed production, it is impossible to breed true to type and variety. It is, as I have discovered, very rare to get a seedling which is 'the very spit' of its parent.

1. Seed Sowing

Various seedsmen offer seeds of the different types of dahlias and particularly of the bedding types. Messrs Thompson & Morgan's catalogue, for instance, offers nineteen different kinds or varieties in packets costing from 5p to 15p. In many cases they point out quite rightly that the varieties are 'variable from seed' or, in some cases, 'come fairly true from seed'. One can buy the seeds of Cactus, Charm, Collarette, Pompon, Orchid-flowered and Mignon Dahlias, and also special strains such as Unwin's Dwarf and Unwin's Ideal Bedder.

The sowing of the seed is done in a similar manner to that for half-hardy annuals, and I recommend using John Innes Seed Compost. To make this up, mix 2 parts (by bulk) medium sterilized loam, 1 part good sedge peat, and 1 part coarse silver sand, adding to each bushel of the mixture $1\frac{1}{2}$ oz superphosphate of lime (16 per cent phosphoric acid), and 1 oz ground limestone or chalk. (This compost can be bought ready mixed.)

Seed boxes of standard size, and made either of wood or of aluminium, should be obtained from a horticultural sundries-man.

Boxes made of wood should be dipped in Rentokil preservative for a few minutes, to protect the wood from attacks by fungus diseases and so prolong the life of the box. The aluminium tray will have holes in the bottom for drainage, and the bottom boards of the wooden seedbox will be slightly apart to allow for the passage of excess moisture. Pieces of broken pot, known as crocks, should be placed over the holes or slits in the bottom of the seedbox. The crocks should then be covered with sedge peat, say half a handful over each, and the box may then be filled with compost. When levelled and pressed down flat the compost should be within an eighth of an inch of the top edge of the box.

Do not vary the proportions of the fertilizers. These should be very strictly adhered to, and not merely approximated but carefully weighed. The same rule applies when measuring soil by bulk. To give a guideline for measurement, 1 bushel of earth will exactly fill a box measuring 22 in. by 10 in. by 10 in. Never make up or buy in more John Innes Seed Compost than you will need for two months.*

Once the John Innes Compost has been levelled and pressed down with a flat wooden presser the dahlia seed may be sprinkled evenly all over the surface. Beginners usually sow the seed too thickly, and so I recommend adding fine silver sand to the seed, 2 parts to 1. The sand can be put into the packet and shaken up with the seed. This makes it easier to sow thinly. Cover the seed with a little more John Innes Seed Compost, using a sieve for best results. A sieve with a fine wire gauze, obtainable from an ironmonger or hardware stores, is ideal for sifting fine soil and sand or compost over seeds sown in boxes.

Once this fine dressing of compost has been sifted over just to cover the seed, another pressing down should be done. Next, a watering should be given through the fine rose of a can, or, if preferred, the box may be dipped very slowly into a large receptacle containing tepid water until the moisture rises up to the top of the soil. Never dip quickly or the water will force up the compost and ruin the careful levelling and sowing that has been done.

* The alternative is to buy the Alex NO-SOIL Compost

The box should then be covered with a clean sheet of glass and also a sheet of brown paper. (Newspaper, in fact, will do, but it looks less tidy.) The box is then ready to be placed on the staging of the greenhouse. The temperature of the greenhouse should be kept between 50 and 60 degrees F. The sheet of glass, incidentally, prevents the compost from drying out too quickly, and the brown paper prevents the sun from shining on the soil. Every morning the sheet of glass should be removed and the 'beads of perspiration' found on the lower side should be wiped off. Some gardeners prefer just to turn the glass over and so save themselves the operation of wiping. The piece of brown paper is put back in position afterwards. The day comes when the seedlings are found to be through the compost, and then the glass and brown paper can be taken off altogether.

It is at this stage that it is advisable to put the boxes or trays on a shelf in the greenhouse quite close to the glass. This is to prevent the seedlings from becoming drawn. It is necessary to keep the compost just moist, and so watering will probably have to continue day by day unless, for some reason, the atmosphere in the greenhouse is humid, in which case watering may only be needed every two or three days. Try to use rain water if possible and not with tap water, especially if the latter is 'limey'.

When the seedlings are 1 in. high they are ready for their first move. Using a short two-prong fork, try to raise each seedling on its own, with a small ball of compost around the roots. The seedlings should go into other seed trays or boxes which have previously been filled with John Innes Potting Compost 2 (particulars of which can be found in the paragraph below). This planting out of baby seedlings is known as pricking off. When pricking off into boxes the rows must be 3 in. apart. Gardeners who have plenty of 3-in. pots may prefer to use these, putting two or three crocks into the bottom of each one, filling them up with John Innes Potting Compost 2, firming with the fingers and then planting one seedling in the centre.

John Innes Potting Compost consists of 7 parts medium sterilized loam, 3 parts good sedge peat, and 2 parts of coarse silver sand. To each bushel of this mixture add 1½ oz hoof and horn meal, 1½ oz superphosphate of lime, ¾ oz sulphate of potash, and 1 oz ground limestone or chalk. This particular formula is known as John Innes Potting Compost 1; for John Innes Potting Compost 2 you merely add twice the quantity of artificial fertilizers and chalk, i.e. 3 oz hoof and horn, 3 oz superphosphate, 1½ oz sulphate of potash, and 2 oz ground limestone or chalk.

Raising New Varieties

This seed sowing method is the one used in raising new varieties. The seed is produced carefully because particular parents are chosen for cross-fertilizing, with the object of eliminating certain characteristics in the varieties and introducing others. To carry out cross-pollination it is necessary to remove all the central disc florets, leaving the ray florets, each with its pistil or female part of the flower. It is on to these pistils that the male pollen of the chosen variety is then placed. The transference is usually done with a camel hair brush, and the flower is covered immediately afterwards with a paper bag, to prevent the bloom being visited by pollinating insects such as bees. (Of course you must thoroughly clean the brush of all pollen before using it again.)

When the special cross has been made, a label is tied on to the stem indicating what has happened. The name of the male variety is stated, the date that the pollen was transferred and, if necessary, the name of the variety of the receptive flower. The male pollen has to be obtained by picking off certain flowers of the selected variety two days before they are wanted and placing them in water. This is the only way to ensure that the pollen is not too dry when it is being used.

Great difficulty is often experienced in getting seed by crossing, owing to the length of time (with doubles) that the bloom takes to mature to the fertile stage, and also to the absence of long sunny periods. In some cases the stigmas in the ray florets are rudimentary, and also these florets have to be pinched off to a certain extent, to prevent damping-off after bagging. Furthermore, these florets often fall out before the seed has 'set'. Therefore, since the chance of self-fertilization is so small, the pollen of the male is transferred to the stigmas of the disc florets of the female. (A careful worker can pull out most, and emasculate those left.) Merely dusting one bloom over the other has often been resorted to, but this is not the best method.

Saving Expense

Seed sowing is also done by gardeners who do not want to go to the expense of buying plants, and who are willing to risk a variation in the height of the plants and the colour of the flowers. I have raised numerous dahlias from seed, and so far I have never been able to guarantee the height of the plants. Another factor is that there will always be a number of singles, although certain seedsmen and nurserymen, it is true, manage to sell seed with a higher proportion of doubles.

Giant Hybrids come fairly true from seed and so do Tom Thumbs. On the whole, however, it is impossible to be certain of heights, and so one cannot plan a border with that beautiful tiered effect which is such a feature of the best dahlia gardens. Collarettes, Decoratives, Cacti, Pompons, and Charms, can all be bought as seed, as can the variety 'Bishop of Llandaff' with its dark foliage and large scarlet flowers, and that almost black-leaved variety 'Queen of Moorland' with its double flowers and dwarf habit.

2. Division of Tubers

Perhaps the simplest method of dahlia propagation is by the division of tubers, but the number of plants that can be produced is strictly limited. Some varieties are more prolific in producing tubers than others. A greater quantity of tubers is obtained, as a rule, when the soil has been properly fed and, above all, mulched with sedge peat. Mulching ensures that moisture is retained in the soil and so helps plump up the underground tubers. Sedge peat should be put on 1 in. deep and in a circle of at least 2 ft across around the plants.

There are two main methods of division. The first is to separate all the tubers (which, of course, will be found at the base of the stored plants) towards the end of April. Each tuber should be perfectly healthy and should have at least one eye or bud (as in the case of potatoes) at its 'proper end', i.e. the end where it was originally joined to the main stem. The healthy tubers are kept in the greenhouse or frame so that they cannot be damaged by frost. They are then planted out separately, with the top of each tuber about 2 in. below soil level. This work is best done about 7 May. The bed should have been lightly forked over beforehand, and a fish manure with a high potash content added at 4 oz to the square yard. If the soil tends to be light the bed should be given a good filling, to firm it. You never get good results if you plant tubers in loose puffy soil. Dahlia varieties grown in this way usually flower about ten days later than plants that have been raised by striking cuttings.

The second, and undoubtedly the better method, is to bring the clusters of tubers (still attached to the stems of last year's plants) into the greenhouse, as if you were going to produce cuttings from them. When the tubers are taken out of winter store they should be placed on shallow boxes filled with damp loose sedge peat, and pressed into the peat so that they are slightly buried. Place the boxes on the staging of the greenhouse, and

Tubers started into growth in the greenhouse in February soon produce new shoots. Note the 'eyes' just appearing at the base of the old stem

So long as there is a shoot and some of the old root, each portion of the divided tuber will make a good plant and will flower until October

keep the temperature at about 60 degrees F. With this moderate heat, and also light watering, the tubers will start to produce young growths. When these shoots are about 1 in. long the tubers should be separated from each other with a sharp knife. Each tuber is severed as near its apex as possible, to ensure that it is bearing one or more shoots.

With 'high crown' varieties it is often necessary to use a hacksaw and cut the crown into sections, leaving areas of surface which are 'alive'. Direct planting is definitely necessary then, especially when one eye is left to each portion.

If the shoots on the tubers are not more than $\frac{1}{4}$ in. long it is possible to plant them out about the beginning of May, each section or portion being spaced out the right distance apart. In the case of dahlias growing 1 ft high, 1 ft apart, in the case of dahlias growing 3 ft high, 3 ft apart, and so on. Because the shoots are only $\frac{1}{4}$ in. long and because they are buried 2 in. deep, the growth will not come through the soil, one hopes, before all danger of a late May frost has passed.

If, on the other hand, the shoots on the tubers are about 1 in. long by the beginning of May, then it pays to pot them up individually into 3-in. pots, using John Innes Potting Compost 1 for the purpose. The pots should then be placed in the greenhouse, or in a heated frame, until the end of May or the beginning of June. The dahlias can then be planted out, the right distance apart, where you want them to flower.

I have sometimes found it necessary to bring dahlia tubers out of their winter storehouse about 15 April. Then, by starting them into growth in the greenhouse, really grand plants have been produced, ready to be put out at the end of May.

3. Grafting

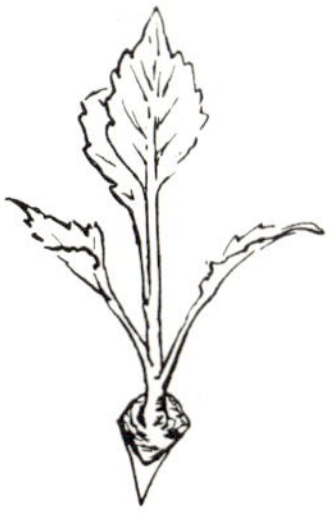

A cutting taken with a small wedge-shaped piece of the parent tuber

If you have become very keen on growing dahlias and have produced new varieties by sowing seeds, you may like to ensure finer plants by grafting some of the young stems of the new variety on to healthy tubers of a well-known strong-growing kind. In this way the stock can be increased and good plants are assured. It is an operation which many nurserymen use when they raise new varieties to sell to the trade and to amateurs.

Dahlia grafting is done on to single tubers, as shown in the drawing. Each tuber is carefully detached from the main cluster of tubers found at the base of the plant, and potted up into a 3-in. pot filled with John Innes Potting Compost 1 or, alternatively, No-Soil Compost 1, which I have used with great success. Both composts can be bought ready for use. The top inch of

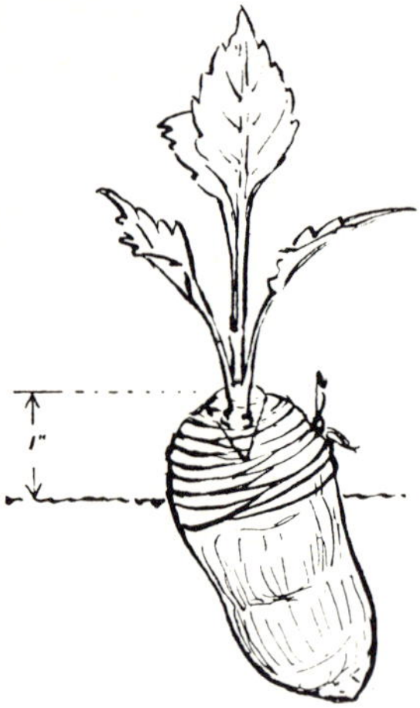

Raffia is tied around for security

the tuber is left exposed, as shown in the drawing, and the wedge-shaped graft is inserted into this top inch. A sharp knife or razor blade is used to make a cut in the tuber, and to cut the base of the young dahlia growth into a wedge shape. This shoot or graft should be not more than 2 in. long, and the bottom leaves should be removed.

After the graft has been inserted the join should be bound fairly tightly with raffia. The pot with its tuber and graft should then be plunged up to its rim in slightly damp sedge peat, inside a box or propagating frame set on the benching of the greenhouse. There must be about 4 in. of head room above the level of the peak, to allow for the growth of the grafted shoot or scion. If a box is used a sheet of glass must be put over the top.

The greenhouse should be heated; this slight bottom heat coming from the hot water pipes or electric tubes will ensure the necessary warmth in the propagating box or frame. Keep the box closed, but every morning remove the glass or open the top of the frame in order to wipe the underside of the glass and expel excess moisture. It may be necessary to give the peat a little tepid water to keep it slightly moist. The complete union between the graft and the cutting of the tuber seldom takes place for three or four weeks. Success depends on maintaining the right balance between dryness and moisture while the grafted tuber is in the propagating box or case.

4. Taking Cuttings

The simplest and most popular way of increasing one's stock of dahlias is by taking cuttings. From one good healthy plant it is possible, with care, to produce six, seven, or even more good plants of the same variety for the following season. Some growers have claimed to do even better than this. One can only get a large number of cuttings if good tubers are produced and if these are stored carefully through the winter.

Because dahlias are tender, the plants are cut down by the first heavy frost in the autumn. Fortunately, however, the tuberous roots will stand a considerable frost providing the land is properly drained. When the soil is sodden the tubers can be more easily frozen. The plants can be cut down to within 3 or 4 in. of soil level a few days after the leaves and flowers have been ruined by a hard frost. In some years this occurs late towards the end of September, but it may be as late as mid November.

Digging up and Labelling Tubers

About four or five days after the tops have been cut down it is time to dig up the tubers very carefully. It is as well to plunge the spade into the soil some distance away from the stem, first one side and then another, in order to bring the plants up whole. In

By using a spade rather than a fork to extricate the well-established roots, you run far less risk of damaging the fat portions of the tuber

this way none of the tubers will be broken off but will all remain attached to the main stem. See that the labelling is done carefully and properly; I find it advisable to use special wax impregnated cardboard labels which do not rot off during the winter. Tie the label firmly to the main stem of each plant as it is dug up.

It may sound peculiar to stress how important this labelling is, but again and again I have had to try and name varieties that have become thoroughly muddled, because the gardener relied on old wooden labels pushed in casually among the tubers stored in their boxes, and somehow when the tubers were transferred to the greenhouses the labels got misplaced. Take great care over labelling, therefore, because when there is only a dead stem and a few tubers it is impossible for an amateur to recognize the varieties.

Winter Storage of Tubers

The tubers should be stored in a shed, room or cellar which is dry and frost-proof. They could be put into boxes by varieties,

Roots that have been lifted and dried will store better if they are prepared for storage by trimming and compacting

With the stem reduced in length to an inch or so and the thin roots cut away, the completed tuber is ready to be stored for the winter

perhaps, or laid on the dry floor covered with a light layer of dry sand, dry sedge peat or dry soil. Care should be taken, however, to see that the crown of the tuber is never covered. Some gardeners believe in storing the plants upside down for a few days, in order to get rid of all excess moisture. If moisture is allowed to collect around the base of the stems this may cause rotting. After a few days the tubers may be turned the right way up.

Whether or not the tubers and stems are turned upside down for several days, the important thing is to ensure that no moisture can collect around the tubers when in store. Far more rotting takes place in winter from dampness than from frost. One year, I remember, frost did get in to the storehouse where I was keeping my tubers, for two consecutive nights, but because the tubers were perfectly dry they were not killed. This does not mean to say that gardeners can afford to be careless about frost. I only mention it to emphasize the importance of making certain that the tubers in storage are never damp. Fungus diseases always strike in moist conditions.

Some people lose their tubers in the winter because of what they call 'fermentation'. This, they say, starts in the stem and works down to the ground. This fermentation is undoubtedly a form of botrytis, which probably starts because of dampness in the store. Be careful not to put the roots in a hot cupboard because then they will shrivel up and become quite useless. Also, don't use warm places that are damp and dark, where new shoots would be forced before outdoor planting is possible. The tubers need to be stored at a temperature just above freezing point, so that when they come into the greenhouse they will be nice and plump.

Avoid the all too common practice of washing soil off tubers, and even, perhaps drying the tubers afterwards with excessive heat. Except in the case of large tuber varieties, this will result in shrivelling and loss.

If mildew appears on the tubers, take care to rub it off so that it doesn't spread to other tubers. I always rub it off with a dry rag, first dipped in a little sulphur dust.

One of the main factors affecting the success of winter storage and the consequent vigour of the plants next season is the quality of previous growth. The tubers will winter well if reserves, including sugar, have been built up in the summer.

Having wintered the tubers successfully, bring them into the greenhouse at the end of January or beginning of February to be started into growth. The nurseryman usually starts taking cuttings soon after Christmas, but the amateur, who does not need to produce so many plants from each root, can wait until well on into February if desired.

A mixture of sedge peat and coarse sand in equal proportions is ideal for rooting dahlia cuttings

Obtaining Cuttings

The tubers should be placed in a box containing enough sedge peat and coarse sand (equal quantities) to bed the tubers, but not to cover their crowns. The crown, called the collar by some growers, is actually the spot where the top end of the tubers joins the old stem, and one reason for leaving it uncovered is that it is then easier to remove the growing shoots when they appear. With varieties that make very large tubers the basal ends of these may be cut back an inch or two so that they take up less room.

Peat is used because it helps to retain moisture and yet lets the air get to the tubers as well. If the sand and peat are thoroughly moistened before the tubers are bedded in, each an inch or so down, there should be no need to give any water for ten days or so. Make sure that this compost is not too wet, or the tubers will rot. Once the little shoots or growths start to appear, more water can be given to keep the tubers moist. When adding water try not to allow any moisture to collect around the crowns. For this reason it is quite important to see that all the tubers in the box are buried at the same depth.

At this time, be sure you do not disturb the labels tied to the stems. Make certain these are above the compost, and re-write them if they are not quite legible.

Experts differ on the subject of cutting back tubers, as mentioned above. Some do this regularly, but others say that new roots always form at the ends or tips of the tubers, and by removing them you get later and lower production of cuttings. They therefore prefer to cut some of the tubers off altogether when they bury the stools in the box.

Tuber pruning is only done, as a rule, with the very full varieties, the Giant Decoratives for instance. With these, if they are grown well, the tubers may easily take up a square foot of space. The amateur who wants to propagate them finds to his horror that they take up an embarrassing amount of room in the greenhouse. One method that can be adopted, in order to save space, is to grow a number of the taller plants as close as 1 ft apart in a spare border which should not be well manured. The plants in this border need not be allowed to flower, and because they are planted close together they only produce quite small tubers. These can be easily dug up after the first frost, dried off and stored. Such tubers take a quarter of the amount of room in the greenhouse and yet, for the amateur, they produce a good number of first class cuttings.

The temperature in the greenhouse at this time should be about 60 to 65 degrees F. If, however, you have only one greenhouse that you are using for all kinds of plants, then the desired temperature of 60 degrees should be that of the propagating frame or box where the cuttings are to be placed. This enables you to have the rest of the house at a temperature of about 50 degrees F. The propagating box needs bottom heat, and this can be provided either by hot water pipes below or by simple wire cable heating below the rooting compost. This latter method is inexpensive and yet very effective. The local Electricity Board will be able to let you have a leaflet on this subject.

To obtain bottom heat, the majority of amateurs still use oil heaters, though unfortunately this is not the most efficient method. And yet our secretary has regularly experienced 95 per cent 'takes', using a small heater with a single burner under the boxed tubers on one staging, and a second, warmer, one under the 'striking' bench. Each bench is covered below the bench level at front and sides with thick material to make sure all the warmth rises. The staging is slatted. All cuttings are placed in 3-in. pots, and these are stood in metal trays full of peat. The moist peat will feel warm to the touch, and will conduct the warmth to the striking medium in the pot. Of course a 'juice' heat should be avoided.

Nine days is the shortest length of time in which 'strikes' will take. It is most important that conditions in the greenhouse should be steady during that time.

Having the cutting in pots, one variety per pot, means that potting on can proceed smoothly. Rooting time varies perhaps five weeks, and if mixed varieties were struck in boxes it would be impossible to empty the boxes and re-use the compost.

A good tuber will easily produce three flushes of shoots: first about five shoots, then eight, then twelve, totalling twenty-five from one tuber. I have had this with 'Rothesay Superb' and 'Golden Heart'. Some varieties will only produce one or two flushes, but this does not follow any pattern. With 'Peter Ramsey', in the Large Decorative section, one can get dozens of shoots from a good tuber. The worst rooters are a separate problem and Large Decoratives do take longer.

Because of the bottom heat young shoots will soon appear, and these should be severed from their parent tubers with a sharp knife when they are 3–4 in. long. Sometimes the very first shoots to appear are rather thick and do not therefore root easily. At other times they are somewhat hollow and then, in my experience, they do not make good plants. The length and size of the cuttings depend to a great extent on the variety; Large-flowered Decoratives tend to produce larger cuttings than Dwarf-bedding Dahlias or Miniature-flowered Cactus Dahlias. In the former case, therefore, the cuttings could be about 3 in. long and in the latter only 2 in.

Some authors have advised that cuttings should be removed with a small piece of the tuber attached. But when this is done the number of cuttings that can be produced is reduced considerably, for at the base of each cutting will be found little eyes or buds, called pips by some gardeners, and it is these that will grow up to form further shoots. Take care, therefore, never to cut too close to the tuber. In fact, see that about $\frac{1}{8}$ in. is left in position. Taking cuttings with a piece of tuber attached invariably results, of course, in numerous stems being produced after the planting out in the flowering bed has been done. Most of us want one good stem, and a number of secondary stems coming up from the roots can be an embarrassment.

If the tuber is plump and healthy then it should be possible to obtain four good cuttings from what seemed originally to be one good bud. It is true that after the first four strong growths have been produced a number of others may grow out which are thin and straggly, but these never make good plants. Now that the

Making a cutting

shoot has been severed from its tuber it can be made into a cutting, first of all by removing the bottom leaves with a sharp blade of a knife and then by making a cut just below a node or a joint. This is the somewhat swollen part on the shoot out of which the young leaves have grown.

Striking Cuttings

Get hold of some well washed 3-in. pots. Put two or three broken crocks in the bottom to ensure good drainage and fill them up to their rims with John Innes Potting Compost 1 or use the special

Cutting ready for insertion, and cuttings potted up

No-Soil Compost made by the Alex Peat Company, Burnham-on-Sea. Some have had good results by mixing coarse silver sand with fine sedge peat in the proportion of one to three. The pots, when filled with one of these composts, should be tapped on the potting shed bench to help the materials settle evenly.

A hole should then be made with a blunt stick about 3 in. long and about twice as thick as a pencil. A little sand should be dropped into the bottom of the hole and the cuttings should then be put in, as shown in the drawing. The compost should then be pressed down lightly around the base of the cutting. Put three cuttings, at equal distances, around the edge of the pot because in this position they will strike more quickly. They get extra air and extra moisture, the sides of the pot being porous. Once the three cuttings are in position water them through the fine rose of a can and place the pot in the propagating box or frame, plunged up to its rim in sedge peat.

Some cuttings will root in twelve days and others may take twenty days. It depends on the variety, on the temperature, and on the time of year. It helps if the frame is shaded from very bright sunshine in the early stages, and if the cuttings are syringed over lightly with tepid water. However long it takes to root (and I have known it take nearly a month), do not attempt to pot up the cuttings into their individual pots until they have grown about ½ in. The exception to the rule is when two cuttings out of the three are at the right stage of growth and the third seems to hang back. In this case I don't wait until all three have rooted because otherwise the first two will be overgrown later on. The cuttings are potted up at the same time, those that have rooted and those that have not, and it is not long before the unrooted specimen, or specimens, send out roots.

Potting Up Cuttings

Once again wash the 3-in. pots, crock them fully, and then fill them with John Innes Potting Compost 2 or No-Soil Compost. Plant the rooted cuttings firmly in the compost, one in the centre of each pot. Keep an eye on the labels during this operation. There must be a label for the three cuttings in their first pot and extra labels when they are rooted and potted up singly.

One or two experts of my acquaintance make up a special dahlia potting compost, consisting of three parts good garden soil (preferably sterilized), one part coarse silver sand and one part spent hops. To every bushel of this mixture is added 2 oz of fish manure and 2 oz of hydrated lime. It is claimed that the spent hops are particularly beloved by dahlia roots, and that when the pot plants are knocked out at planting time, towards the end of May, the ball of soil holds together far better than when sedge peat is used. I have no experience of this but mention it because it is often discussed when dahlia growers meet together.

Once the dahlias have been potted up singly they can be placed on the staging of the greenhouse at a temperature of about 45 degrees F, or they can be put on the shelving of the greenhouse, near the light and out of the way. From now on the aim is to harden them off gradually so that they will be fit to plant out. I will return later to the subject of hardening off.

No-Soil Compost

I have had very good results, in recent years, with No-Soil Compost. This is made up from special sedge peat, coarse silver sand, and the necessary plant nutrients. Sufficient plant foods are incorporated with the sedge peat and silver sand to make an excellent seedling compost. Extra plant nutrients are provided in a special sachet so that the user can convert the seedling compost into Potting Composts 1, 2 and 3 in a few moments.

Hormone Helps

Some of us, like my wife, have green fingers, and so have no difficulty in propagating dahlias. Others do not find it so easy! When this is so, there is nothing shameful about using one of the root-forming hormones which can be obtained from any good retail chemist. These special hormones can be bought in powder or liquid form. As soon as the cutting has been prepared it should be dipped into a hormone solution made up in accordance with the instructions on the container. If a liquid is used, the base of the cutting is dipped into it to a depth of $\frac{1}{4}$in., and similarly if you prefer to use a powder. It is said that it is always better to do this in the evening and then allow the cuttings to lie in a cool place before dibbling them into the compost early the following morning. And yet I have had quite good results, using hormones, when dibbling in the cuttings at any time of day, providing that once they are in their propagating box or frame they are shaded from hot sun.

Some of the firms that manufacture this hormone liquid or dust offer a free booklet, giving detailed instructions as to their use. Do not believe people who say that if you use these hormones good tubers will not be produced at the end of the season.

This is an 'old wives' tale' and has no foundation of fact. The only precaution I take, when using hormones, is to rub my hands thoroughly first of all with a barrier cream because I would not like growth promoting substances on my skin. This may be an unnecessary precaution but I prefer it that way.

Cuttings in Boxes

When there is little space in the greenhouse, when the gardener has become expert at cutting production, or when hormones are used to ensure an almost 100 per cent 'take', seed boxes can be used for cuttings instead of 3-in. pots. The standard size boxes which can be bought from any horticultural sundriesman are 14 in. long, $8\frac{1}{2}$ in. wide and 3 in. deep. These are often called 'seed trays', and are supplied either ready made up or in sets of wood cut to the right size to be nailed together by the gardener. If these seed trays are dipped in Rentokil preserving liquid for ten minutes or so they will last a long time. Latterly I have been using aluminium trays, of the same size, which of course last almost for ever!

The rooting compost is placed in these trays and the cuttings are then dibbled in 2 in. apart with the rows 3 in. apart or, if preferred, 2 in. square. They are lightly firmed, well watered with tepid water through the fine rose of a can, and placed in the propagating case. One can usually get twenty-five cuttings into a box, which makes the final counting easier. Keep a notebook with a page for each variety, and then each time a cutting is taken of a particular variety, make a record on the appropriate page. (Remember also to provide a label.) I thus can make sure that I take sufficient cuttings of each variety, with perhaps a few over in case of losses.

Using the Staging

Some of my friends put sheets of asbestos on the staging of their small greenhouse, and then nail together strips of planking 6 in. wide to form a bottomless box fitting exactly over the area occupied by the sheeting. Coarse sifted ashes are placed 1 in. deep on the sheeting and on top of this a 3-in. layer of compost. When the compost has been watered and pressed down with a wooden presser, the cuttings are dibbled in in rows 2 in. apart, allowing only 1 in. between the rows. A large pane of glass, such as is used for a Dutch Light, is then placed over the top and thus a large propagating frame is produced into which the cuttings may go until they are rooted and ready for potting up. In this way the compost is used again and again for cutting production until the year's run of dahlia cuttings is completed.

Vermiculite

There is a special sterile mica product which is sold in the shops as Vermiculite. It contains, of course, no plant foods at all but it does hold moisture. Many people therefore use it for striking dahlia cuttings. There are two things against Vermiculite, first the expense and second the fact that the cuttings must be removed immediately the roots have been produced, or they tend to hang fire and in fact 'go back'. I always prefer to use sedge peat because of its humus content and because it is an organic product.

Soil Blocks and Alternative Pots

Today there are a number of little machines on the market, some of them expensive and others less so, which can be used for making soil blocks of John Innes Potting Compost 1. These blocks are so pressed together by the machine that they do not fall apart when watered. During the making they are provided with a hole in the centre, ½in. wide and about 1 in. deep, and so the dahlia cuttings can be inserted into these holes once they have grown some roots or, as the gardener puts it, once they have struck.

Some soil block makers produce a cylindrical cast about 3in. in diameter and 3in. high, others produce them with a hexagonal shape. In both cases the amount of John Innes Compost contained in the soil block is about twice as much as can be placed in a 3-in. pot. Those who use these soil blocks claim (a) that you do not have to buy any pots and therefore the cost of the block making machine is repaid again and again, and (b) that because there is no porous pot to evaporate the moisture, less watering has to be done. Also, since there is more soil, the fast-rooting little dahlia plant likes it better.

One has to be careful not to break off all the roots from a cutting, when potting up into the small hole in the centre of a soil block, and so I find it best to put up soon after the cutting has struck, while the roots are quite small. Having put the base of the cutting in the centre of the hole, pour some of the same compost out of a cupped hand into the soil block hole to fill it. Then all you have to do is to press down lightly with both thumbs, to make the soil you have poured into the hole just firm. If you leave a little depression at the top it makes for easy watering.

Special pots are available, made of 75 per cent peat and 25 per cent cellulose fibre. These are known as jiffy pots and can be said to combine the advantages of soil blocks and clay pots. They can be bought in various sizes: $1\frac{1}{4}$ in. square, $2\frac{1}{4}$ in. round, $2\frac{1}{4}$ in. square, 3 in. round, 3 in. square, 4 in. round (the standard pot) and 4 in. square (the azalea pot). (The purpose of square pots is to save considerable space on the greenhouse benching or shelving, and in the frames before planting out.) These peat pots are very cheap indeed and, of course, when the dahlia is planted in the soil where it is to flower, it is not knocked out of the pot but planted pot and all. The pot then decomposes and feeds the plant as well as letting the roots through.

On the whole there is more rapid, properly balanced growth in these pots than in any other, and not only is heating fuel therefore saved but also bench space. There is no planting check at planting time, and losses due to breakage are, of course, eliminated. These jiffy pots are light and easy to handle, and are stronger, I find, than any other peat pots I have met with. They should be planted at a depth which brings the level of the pot just below soil level, and there should be no gaps between the pot and the surrounding soil.

Of course it is necessary to keep dahlias in jiffy pots well watered, before they are planted out, but then this has to be done with any other pot. The only thing against these peat pots is that you cannot plunge them in sedge peat, as you can clay pots, to save watering, but in fact very few gardeners are able to do this when they are growing a number of dahlias. Once the dahlias are well established, however, it will be found that they require less watering than when in clay pots, and certainly less than in those black paper pots which some firms sell.

The Hardening-off Process

It is not too difficult to get dahlia cuttings to strike in coarse silver sand, in vermiculite or in a mixture of sedge peat and silver sand. It is not too difficult, either, to pot up the plants in their clay pots, peat pots or soil blocks. Most beginners are able to grow the plants on the staging of the greenhouse, or, better still, on a shelf near the glass, but what does seem to prove difficult and what is not properly understood is the correct process of hardening up. The dahlia grower knows he cannot put his plants into the open garden until all fear of frost is past. In the south this may be after 20 May, but in parts of the north it may not be until 7 June.

The plants, therefore, tend to be hanging about for quite a long time and something must be done with them to keep them growing slowly and sturdily until they can be planted in the open. They cannot be kept in the greenhouse because there will be no room, and also because it is dangerous to plant out the dahlias straight from a warm house into the open. They must therefore go into a deep frame where they can go on growing very slowly with the protection of the glass surround. This moving out into frames for a number of weeks is the beginning of the hardening-off process. I would like to be able to tell the beginner that he could do without a cold frame for dahlias, but unfortunately it is not true.

A great deal can be done with the wire glass frames known as access frames, although they cannot keep out as much frost as a well built frame. You can make do with access frames if you are willing to cover over the glass with plastic sheeting the moment there is any sign of frost, to block up the air spaces, and, when the frost is severe, if you also use some sacks at night-time. Such ingenuity will get you over a difficulty, but in the long run, and for this particular purpose, a frame is best.

Even when a frame is used it is necessary to be careful. If it is warm during the day, for instance, the frame must be open to give plenty of ventilation. As it cools down in the mid-afternoon the frame will have to be closed in order to conserve the heat and thus keep out the frost. When there is a very bad frost for days it is necessary to keep the frame shut tight, as also when there is a bad fog, for fog too will harm the dahlias. The unfortunate thing is that when you do keep the frame tight shut you have to begin the hardening-off process all over again!

As the days go by it should be possible to increase the ventilation steadily, during the day. At night the frame must be shut up, and in addition shutting up sacks may be needed over the glass to give extra protection. The time will come, however, about the third week of May, when it may be possible to leave the glass light well open during the night. Later on, of course, the glass may be taken off all together. In this way the plants get used to the ordinary temperature out of doors so that when they are planted up there is no set-back at all.

It is even possible, when dahlias are grown in clay pots, to make a hole with a trowel and plant the dahlia still in its pot. A few days later, when the compost and clay pot are at the same temperature as the earth around, the plant can be knocked out of its pot and planted in the hole provided.

I am sorry to have spent so much time on this business of hardening-up, but every year hundreds of plants are ruined in the early stages because they are planted out while still quite soft, that is, straight from the greenhouse into the open ground!

Heating the Frame

If the greenhouse is heated by hot-water pipes, it should be possible to take a 2-in. pipe into the frame or frames so that it travels around the inside (a flow and return, as it is called). With oil-fired central heating in the main house it is not too expensive, perhaps when this apparatus is installed, to ask the engineers to see to it that some of the piping heats the greenhouse and part of the frame. In this case one ought to site the greenhouse close to the house to save piping. Because the garage is often heated in this way, to keep the frost out, a greenhouse could perhaps be built on to the back of the garage.

Another method of heating the frame is by using electrical wiring. The wire is buried 6 in. or so below soil level. Ask your local Electricity Board for advice on this subject, because it is important to have the fittings just right.

Potting On

Despite the fact that the keen dahlia grower does everything possible to keep his young plants growing slowly, it is possible, in the case of cuttings that were struck early, that certain varieties produce too many roots for the pots long before the local climate allows the gardener to plant in the open. The result is that the plants tend to get pot-bound. This means that the roots curl round and round in a complete ball beside the pot and seem to 'consume' all the soil or compost there is. These plants, of course, suffer badly in the long run. Eventually the roots get so twisted around one another that they cannot possibly be straightened out at planting time.

It is necessary, therefore, to keep a sharp watch on the earlier struck plants. If the 3-in. pots get too full of roots then the dahlia plants concerned must be potted on into 5-in. pots, this time adding John Innes Potting Compost 3, but first ensuring that the pots are well washed and crocked. All this, of course, makes for extra work, while in addition the 5-in. pots take up far more room in the frame. You will probably prefer, therefore, to strike your dahlia cuttings later, at about the end of March, rather than very early, and so avoid having to 'pot on'.

Storing Tubers Out of Doors

On page 29 I discussed the digging up of tubers in the late autumn or early winter, for storage. If you do not have a convenient cellar or storehouse you may be glad to know that it is possible to store tubers successfully out of doors, in a deep pit in the ground. The idea is to bury them so deep that the frost cannot reach them. It is vital, of course, to have a perfectly drained site, because the tubers must never be allowed to remain in sodden soil.

Choose a spot if possible which is under trees, and here dig a pit 3ft deep and of sufficient length and width to store the Dahlia tubers you wish to keep. It doesn't matter if they have to be placed one on top of the other. The great thing is to be certain that there is at least 18in. of soil above the roots. Some people, instead of covering the tubers with soil, use sedge peat instead, and this of course is not wasted because it can be used afterwards for making into the John Innes Compost.

Label each plant carefully with a plastic label, wire this label on to the stems of the tubers with a plastic covered wire, and use a sharp pencil. Then, when you get the tubers up in the new year, the labelling will still be firm. Only store perfectly healthy tubers. Do not bother to dust them with lime or sulphur, but handle them carefully so that they are not bruised or cut, and bury them properly at the right depth.

4 Preparing and Feeding the Soil

Most gardeners have to put up with whatever soil their garden contains. Those who live near Aldershot may have to cope with almost pure sand. Others who live in London may find it a great bore to prepare the very heavy London clay. Gardeners in Dover will bemoan the very shallow soil they have over chalk. It is customary for gardeners to grumble. When one cannot grumble about the weather or the seed it is always nice to have the soil to grouse at. If I was asked to name the ideal soil for gardeners, I would say a sandy loam. A loam is said to be the ideal mixture between clay and sand, and so a sandy loam is one that has more sand in it than clay.

No dahlia grower, however, need be disheartened because dahlias are not particular as regards soil. I have seen them growing in every part of Great Britain and in many parts of Canada, Rhodesia, South Africa and Europe. The great thing, of course, as in the case of other crops, is to ensure that the land is rich in humus, and that means it is necessary to incorporate into the soil every year plenty of rotted composted vegetable refuse. The details of this appear later in the chapter, under the heading *Correct Manuring and Feeding*.

I have learnt, during the last forty years, that soils can be improved by applying the compost above rather than below. For instance, if you have to cope with very heavy clay in your garden, you will do very little good by digging the well-rotted compost or sedge peat into about 18 in. of soil. You will do far better to fork up the top 6 in. and plant your dahlia tubers in this, and then apply the compost or sedge peat as a part dressing afterwards. If you are one of those who have to cope with shallow soil over chalk, do not, whatever you do, dig down deeply into the soil. Once again, fork down about 4 in. only and then work in the old compost or sedge peat at two bucketfuls to the square yard. Apply one bucketful as a top dressing after planting. If I had to condemn one soil for dahlias it would be chalky soil.

Gardeners with clay soil are always jealous of those who are lucky enough, as they say, to have well-drained sandy soil. But the sands do dry out very quickly and they present a real problem because they are so lacking in humus. In my father's garden at Farnborough, Hants, it was necessary to ram the soil down as firmly as possible, without doing any digging at all, and then plant the dahlia tubers in the sand so that they were just buried. The bed was then covered all over with old compost or damped sedge peat.

The good loam or sandy loam does not present much of a problem to the dahlia grower because it is neither too heavy nor too light. It is not sodden like a clay soil or over dry like a sandy soil, and it is not too acid, as are the peaty soils you sometimes come across in Somerset, parts of Lancashire and Cheshire, Lincolnshire and so on.

Besides difficulties over the soil, some gardeners may have to deal with what are called 'pans'. These are solid layers 2 or 3 in. thick, and perhaps 18 in. down. These 'pans' usually consist of some kind of iron stone, usually with a certain amount of aluminium salts as well, and over the years a layer of cement has formed.

In Cheshire these pans are known as 'fox bench', because it is said that foxes always burrow under them and feel safe. They are bad for the plants because they prevent the downward movement of roots, and the upward movement of worms. If, during your weeding and excavations, you do come across a pan, get hold of a crowbar and plunge it into the ground every 2 or 3 ft, to break up the pan. It is not too thick or hard, as a rule, for this to be done quite easily.

Lime

It may be that lime should be added to the soil. Any soil containing less than one part of lime in 200 parts of soil cannot be brought into a high state of fertility for dahlias. Lime corrects undesirable soil conditions and is also a positive soil-improving agent, providing the calcium needed by the plants as a food. With heavy soil it improves the texture by making it more friable and workable, and with acid soil it counteracts the acidity, which is unfavourable to the growth of good dahlia plants enables the micro-organisms to work in an unrestricted manner, thus ensuring the right decomposition of organic matter, and it also helps release potash and soil phosphates.

To discover the amount of lime to use, the gardener should

buy a special green liquid with which to test the soil. It is made by British Drug Houses and is obtainable from any good chemist. The degree of acidity of the soil is expressed in what to the amateur may seem a mysterious notation: pH7* represents the neutral point, and with figures below 7 indicating the degree of acidity and figures above 7 indicating the degree of alkalinity.

I found that in Great Britain the extremes usually run between pH8.5 and pH4.5. On the whole dahlias do best at about pH6.5. The soil indicator fluid, when soil is added, will either remain green, or turn various shades of yellow, or become orange or red. The chart provided with the bottle of fluid will tell you that bright red is about p4.5 or 5 and a light yellow about pH6. If the fluid remains a dark green then it is either neutral or alkaline. Excess of lime can cause trouble as much as acidity, for the yellowing of the leaves, which gardeners usually call the chloritic condition of the leaves, is brought about by excess of lime. It is therefore called lime-induced chlorosis, and is very common on the chalky lands of Kent.

There is always a certain loss of lime each year, more from sandy soils than from clay, which is why sandy soil is often very acid. In Devon, for instance, where I used to garden, the loss of lime through drainage could be as much as 6 cwt per acre, while in addition the crops themselves could easily use up 1 cwt per acre. There are, of course, different kinds of lime one can use, but dahlia growers will be satisfied with using carbonate of lime which can be bought in bags from a good horticultural sundriesman. This may be applied from 3 oz to 8 oz to the square yard, depending on the acidity of the soil as indicated by the soil test.

Texture

Some people dig heavy soil in the late autumn and leave it rough until the spring. The spadefuls of soil should be left in their clods, so that the frosts, thaws and cold winds can act on these clods and break them down. Thus, when you come to fork the land over in the spring, to make it level, the work will be very easy to do because nature itself has taken a hand. The alternative is to make plenty of good powdery compost with your vegetable waste and apply this as a top dressing on the soil in the early winter. The worms then work on the soil, tunnelling up and down, and so in the spring the land is ready to fork over.

Drainage

Sometimes a householder takes over a new garden where the

* See also pages 160 and 161

land is really sodden and needs drainage. The dahlia will not do well in such soil for it hates being waterlogged. The only answer to such a problem is to dig a well 3–4 ft square at one of the bottom corners of the garden, and then put down 4 in. agricultural drains in a line, with other smaller drains 'radiating' from this row. These drains will will probably only need to be about 18 in. deep, and over them should be placed plenty or coarse coal ashes or clinkers. As a result the excess water from the soil will drain into the clay pipes provided and travel down to the well.

Where drainage has to be done on a fairly large scale it is as well to discuss the case with a county land-drainage officer. In order to make it worthwhile preparing special bed, in wet soils, for dahlias, some gardeners have excavated the ground for 3 ft or so, and buried down below a 1-ft layer of clinkers, old tin cans and other hard rubbish, to produce good drainage. The soil has then been put back over the top.

Correct Manuring and Feeding

When applying manures and organic fertilizers to the soil one is aiming not only to feed the plants, but also to satisfy the needs of the great population of micro-organisms in the soil. The keen dahlia grower will want to encourage the earthworms, particularly, for they will do the cultivation for him and help produce the perfect up and down soil structure which dahlias appreciate so much.

Whatever organic matter is applied it should be in a fully-composted form. It will then assist in the aeration of the soil as well as helping to produce a better physical condition. It is organic matter that brings about the production of humus, which is all-important for healthy growth. Further, dahlias grown on land that has been regularly enriched with fully-rotted organic matter, never suffer seriously from pests and diseases like plants grown on soil deficient in humus. One should therefore fork in properly made compost, which is a richer and more lasting substance than real farmyard manure alone, and is also balanced and foolproof.

Farmyard Manure The term farmyard manure is used to cover both pure cow manure and a mixture of cow and pig manure. Horse manure is kept separate from the other two animal faeces.

Fresh animal manure, when dug in, may have a harmful effect on the soil, because the bacteria which should be doing the day-to-day job of manufacturing nitrogen and releasing it will be busying themselves with trying to break down the fresh straw, and so will be using up the nitrogen in the ground for this purpose. This is called denitrification, and plants growing in soil which is being denitrified can suffer very badly. If, therefore, you are going to buy in farmyard manure or horse manure it should be at least three years old, and should have been properly stored, preferably under cover, in a manure shed.

Sewage I am sometimes asked whether there is any value in the solid matter left behind in cesspools and sewerage tanks. The answer is that it is of little value, for the plant foods lie in the liquid portion which escapes. The Good Gardeners' Association, however, has a committee which works to encourage Town Councils to compost sewage wastes correctly. When this is done gardeners are able to buy plenty of suitable manure at a cheap rate. This not only helps garden soils, but also relieves the rates. If you wish to obtain this excellent organic manure, write to the town clerk of your city or town council and make enquiries.

Seaweed, Shoddy and Spent Hops There is a lot to be said for seaweed. When rotted down on its own it is almost as good as well-rotted compost, and although it contains scarcely any phosphates, it does contain much more potash than farmyard manure. Also, undoubtedly, it contains many different types of trace elements, i.e. minute quantities of certain plant foods, which can make all the difference. It is free from weed seeds and plant diseases, and decomposes very rapidly in the soil. Once it is rotted down it can be dug into the soil in the autumn at the rate of one good barrel load to 10 square yards. It can be used with great effect on the compost heap, as an activator.

Wool shoddy and cotton shoddy are waste products often obtainable by gardeners living in the north of England. Both unfortunately, take a long time to rot down and their value depends on the fineness of the division and on the nitrogen content. The best shoddy comes from pure wool. It can be dug in during the autumn when the ground is being prepared, at the rate of 1 lb to the square yard. Some northern dahlia growers who have light soil have told me that they like shoddy because it tends to act as a sponge and hold the moisture.

Dwarf bedding dahlia, 'Red Flash'

Some firms, particularly in London, offer spent hops as a substitute for farmyard manure. Spent hops are a by-product of

brewing, and are rich in nitrogen, which of course feeds the leaves, but low in phosphates and potash. If they are used, bone meal and wood ashes must be applied in addition.

Sedge Peat This is quite different from sphagnum peat, though they are sold at similar prices. Sedge peat contains about 200 lb per ton of immediately available humus and sphagnum peat only about 45 lb. Sedge peat usually contains 141 lb of nitrogen (expressed as sulphate of ammonia) and sphagnum peat only 70 lbs. Sedge peat has additional humus finally available in the region of 70 per cent, while in the case of sphagnum peat it is seldom more than 15 per cent. Those who have small gardens and so cannot make large quantities of compost should buy in sedge peat and fork it into the ground at two bucketfuls to the square yard. It is possible to use a properly balanced fish manure in addition, containing 6 per cent nitrogen, 6 per cent potash and 6 per cent sulphate at 3 to 4 oz to the square yard.

In addition to being forked in, sedge peat can always be applied as a top dressing, to act as a mulch. It is ideal for dahlias, being neither too alkaline nor too acid and containing no weed seeds. It should be applied around the plants to a width of 2 ft or more and a depth of 1 in., early in June. It will give the dahlias just the conditions they require.

Green Manure Gardeners who cannot get hold of sufficient vegetable waste can consider increasing the humus in the soil by adding what is called green manure. This is obtained by growing certain plants and then, before they come to manurity, digging them into the ground quite shallowly. Mustard, rye, vetches, and annual lupins are often used, the seed being well crossed in the sowing. The plants that result are dug in two or three months later. Some gardeners sow all the seeds they have left over towards the end of the season and then dig in the plants that grow up, *en masse*, for green manure.

If green manuring is to be carried out there are three things to be borne in mind: (1) that the land to be green manured must be free and available for at least three good growing months; (2) that before the green crops are dug into the soil they must be well crushed with a spade, and (3) that a fish manure should be applied over the crushed material at 4 oz to the square yard, to prevent the green manure from denitrifying the soil.

Prospective dahlia growers who have to face a plot of land that is full of perennial weeds may like to try the double green

'Crystello'

manuring method. The land is dug over shallowly in early winter and left until early spring, and then the seeds of tares should be sown broadcast at the rate of $\frac{1}{2}$oz to the square yard. In June, the tares should be knocked down thoroughly with a spade and fish manure applied at 3oz to the square yard. The bed should then be left for eight days, after which the crushed crop should be dug in in the normal manner. The surface of the soil should then be lightly cultivated once more, with rye grass sown at the rate of 1oz to the square yard. This rye should be dug into the ground in late October or early November, having first been treated with fish manure as were the tares. The disadvantage of this system is that it entails giving up a plot of land for a whole year, and so it will only be adopted where the ground is foul with weeds and lacking humus.

The alternative to using the double green manuring method is to apply one or more of the special hormone weed killers which will kill most weeds. More details of these weed killers are given at the end of this chapter.

Making a Compost Heap

In every garden some odd corner, preferably one protected from the wind and excess rain or sun, should be set aside where vegetable waste can be collected and placed on a heap day by day, week by week. Gardeners living on the coast can also collect and use seaweed. Ideally the heap will be 6ft square. To provide a frame for it, drive in 4 stout posts and nail boards to these posts, on three sides. Gaps of 1in. should be left between the boards, and all the wood should be protected with Rentokil preservative.

Fresh green material, such as grass cuttings and green leaves, should be added in thin layers of 1 to 2in. with 4- or 5-in. layers of bulkier material, such as straw or the stalks of herbaceous plants, in between. The softer material helps to rot down the more woody substances.

After every 6-in. layer of vegetable refuse collected in this way a good fish manure* should be sprinkled on, at 3oz per square yard. It may be days before the next 6-in. layer is achieved or, because some crop like potatoes is being harvested, it may be arrived at in one day or sooner!

Where it is possible to obtain the excreta of poultry or rabbits this should go on to the heap also. Once a week or so, if the weather is dry, the heap may be given a good watering. Care

* Or seaweed manure

should be taken to keep the heap moist but not saturated, and when it gets to 3 or 4 ft high a fork may be plunged into it at two or three places to aerate it.

Such vegetable waste should be ready to use in about 6 months. It is convenient, therefore, to have two heaps going, one which is almost ready to use and the other which is being piled up for use in about six months' time. To keep the material from blowing about in a windy spot run wire netting over each heap.

Some gardeners prefer to dig pits* and rot the material in these. The advantage of this system is that the material is never unsightly, and also it gets all the water it needs in rainy weather, but the disadvantage is that the material has to be dug out afterwards, often from some depth.

When ready the compost should be dark brown or almost black in colour and quite free from any objectionable smell. It then serves as a source of energy for the development of various beneficial organisms in the soil. Such humus has been said to be 'dynamic', and from the point of view of the plants, it certainly is.

Composting is one of the most important pieces of work in the garden. Don't waste any vegetable matter, please!

Organic Fertilizers

Once the dahlia grower has realized the importance of digging in compost, sedge peat or other suitable organic substances, he may supplement these with organic fertilizers. With dahlias I have found that it pays to concentrate on phosphates, which will help with root formation, and on potash, which helps to give firmness to stems and solidity to plants. Dahlias are naturally succulent in their growth, so it is never advisable to over-do nitrogenous fertilizers which only encourage luxuriant foliage and rampant growth. Furthermore, plants that have been given too much nitrogen invariably produce blooms lacking in colour.

It is true that the three main plant foods needed are nitrogen, phosphates and potash, but these must be supplied in the right proportions and it is quite useless to apply one of the substances in excess in the hope that it will make up for the deficiency of another. Their effects are quite distinct: nitrogen works mainly to build up the stems and green leaves of the plant, phosphates strengthen the roots and help produce steady, continuous and firm growth, which is most valuable, and potash plays an important part in the production of firm plants with highly-coloured flowers. Potash is normally deficient in sandy soils.

* This is popular in Australia

Nitrogen The most commonly used organic nitrogenous fertilizers are:

1. Dried Blood. This contains 12 to 15 per cent nitrogen and is quite a quick-acting fertilizer. It is best applied before planting, since it usually takes about seven days before the bacteria release the plant nutrients. It may be used dry, and left to be washed in by the rain, or it may be watered in. Apply it at the rate of 2 to 3 oz to the square yard.

2. Soot. This contains a very small percentage of nitrogen, usually less than 1 per cent. It is therefore a very mild type of plant food and can be used at the rate of 6 to 7 oz to the square yard. Used fresh it may give a little trouble from 'fumes', so I usually allow it to stand for three months or so before applying it.

Phosphates The most commonly used organic phosphatic fertilizers are:

1. Steamed Bone Flour. This is fairly slow-acting and is usually applied at the rate of 2 to 3 oz to the square yard, in the autumn.

2. Bone meal. This is even slower in action and is generally applied at 3 to 4 oz to the square yard.

Potash The chief organic potassic fertilizers are:

1. Wood Ashes. They contain about 7 per cent potash and are usually applied at 6 to 8 oz to the square yard.

2. Flue dust. This contains up to 10 per cent potash as a rule and may be applied at 4 to 5 oz to the square yard.

Compound Organic Fertilizers

There are a number of compound organic fertilizers which are used with success by gardeners. The composition of these fertilizers may be either natural, as in the case of bird guano, or purposely regulated as in the case of a fish fertilizer.

Hoof and Horn Meal This contains 12 to 14 per cent nitrogen, 4 to 5 per cent phosphates and, if sulphate of potash is added during preparation, 5 to 10 per cent potash. It is usually applied at 3 to 4 oz to the square yard and is excellent in John Innes Seed and Potting Composts.

Meat and Bone Meal This usually contains up to 10 per cent nitrogen and up to 30 per cent phosphoric acid. When such an organic fertilizer is compounded, an ex-organic form of sulphate of potash is often added, giving about 5 per cent potash. This is quite a good organic fertilizer to use in the garden a fortnight or so before planting out the dahlias.

Fish Fertilizers Fish manures are excellent for soil fertility. They may contain 6 to 10 per cent nitrogen, 5 to 8 per cent phosphoric acid, and 2 to 3 per cent potash. If more sulphate of potash is added it is possible to produce a first-class fish fertilizer with 10 per cent potash. The great advantage of fish manure is that it contains other trace elements.

There is a second type of fish fertilizer which contains 6 per cent nitrogen, 6 per cent phosphates and 6 per cent potash. It is usually applied at 3 to 4 oz to the square yard a week or ten days before putting out the plants. It may also be used as a top dressing in midsummer, at a similar rate. If the weather is dry it can be watered in well afterwards.

Bird Guano This consists of the excreta of birds and sea animals, as well as the dead bodies of birds, rats and seals. Material that has accumulated on small islands in rainless and arid regions usually contains about 10 per cent nitrogen, 10 per cent phosphates and 4 per cent potash, with traces of other minerals. This is an excellent manure, and quick-acting. It is therefore usually applied just before planting, or even ten days later, at 2 to 3 oz to the square yard. Unfortunately it is now rather expensive and difficult to get hold of.

Special Hints about Manuring Dahlias

With light sandy soils it is important to incorporate plenty of well-rotted compost or sedge peat, to provide the necessary humus to help hold the moisture. (It is a good idea to dampen the sedge peat before adding it to sandy soils.) This fine organic matter should be forked in at a rate of at least one large bucketful per square yard plus a good fertilizer, for instance a fish fertilizer with a 10 per cent potash content at 3 to 4 oz to the square yard. Further sedge peat could be given later, as a top dressing after planting, to act as a mulch.

In the case of the heavier soils, or of any good garden soil that has been well manured for years, it may only be necessary to fork in good old compost or medium grade sedge peat at half a bucketful to the square yard, and to add a fish manure with a 6 per cent potash content at 3 oz to the square yard.

It is not advisable to dig in a heavy dressing of fresh animal manure before planting. This would encourage rank growth and the production of too much foliage. If old farmyard manure can be obtained it would be better to use it as a top dressing around the plants at the end of July and the beginning of August. For it is at this time of the year that dahlias do appreciate a little extra organic nitrogen plus a mulch surface.

It is always better to apply properly composted vegetable waste than dung for it is more valuable to the soil and to plants.

If you do not like using a fish manure, apply a meat and bone meal instead at 3 oz to the square yard, plus wood ashes, for example at $\frac{1}{2}$ oz to the square yard, or one of the flue dusts at 5 oz to the square yard.

During the growing season plant foods can be given in the form of a properly balanced liquid manure if the plants seem to be lagging behind. Liquid manures are easily available and should be used in accordance with the directions on the labels. There is a type of liquid manure which is specially made up for flower feeding, compounded of organic substances and containing the right proportions of phosphates and potash. Liquid plant foods are, of course, taken up almost immediately by the dahlias, and they thus ensure quick results.

Hormone Weed Killers

A house owner is sometimes unfortunate enough to take over a garden which has been badly neglected by a previous owner, or which is just part of a rough field. In such land there may easily be pernicious perennial weeds such as docks, creeping thistle, creeping buttercup, and couch or twitch grass. It is not easy to eliminate these weeds completely by digging, forking or hoeing, and therefore it is useful to know that they can be eliminated with hormone weed killers.

Perhaps the strongest of these is SBK (which contains 2:4.D and 2:5.D). SBK will destroy thistles, docks, nettles, bindweed, brambles, and even the old stumps of trees. It must be used before the garden is planted up, because it will kill rose bushes, shrubs, perennials and the like. It will not, however, get rid of grass weeds like couch and twitch, and in this case Dowpon should be used. This contains Dalapon, a sodium salt, and may be applied to the blades of growing grasses when they are about 4 in. high. Dowpon should never be applied when rain is expected within twelve hours. Besides killing couch or sctuch Dowpon will also eliminate wild oats, oxtails, perennial grasses such as the black or creeping bent, reeds, and bracken.

Any readers who find any difficulty in getting hold of these two excellent weed killers may write to me for names and addresses of suppliers. It is best to use these weed eliminators at the first opportunity and get rid of the weeds completely. Then, after six months, the gardener may start, so to speak, with a clean slate.

5 Planting Dahlias

When to plant

It is never advisable to plant dahlias in the open garden before all fear of frost is over. This usually means that one cannot plant until 20 May in the south, or the first week of June in the colder parts of the north. There are, of course, exceptions to every rule, and readers who are lucky enough to live in the sheltered parts of Cornwall will be able to plant far earlier than gardeners who live on the east coast of Yorkshire. On the other hand there are parts of the north-west coast of Scotland which are considerably warmer and more sheltered than, say, the east coast of Norfolk.

The great thing is to know one's district well and so not be guided by dates alone. There can be particularly warm spells early in May which tempt unwary beginners to plant early, much to their disgust later on when a serious frost occurs. The advantage of planting early is that the dahlias bloom earlier – there is no doubt about that. Because they bloom early they will have a very long flowering season. In fact in some years, in my garden, I have had them in flower until late October, and looking very beautiful too.

Growers, therefore, who are most anxious to get early flowers, either because they need cut blooms long before their neighbours or because they want them for some particular show, try to get the planting done early in May. They then cover the dahlias with large lantern-like cloches, or with square glass Access frames, for protection. Generally speaking frosts are not too severe in May and so cloches, or Access frames, which can keep out 5 or 6 degrees of frost, give first-class protection.

Some writers have said that to plant early means that the dahlias themselves are rather exhausted by the end of the season and that you cannot, so to speak, burn the candle at both ends. This is not so, however, in my experience. It is of course necessary to feed regularly, it is important to mulch, and it helps greatly if the dead flowers of the dahlias are picked off regularly. One year I cut back a number of the earliest flowering varieties quite hard, that is to say within a foot of soil level, early in September, and by the end of October they had grown up again and were flowering very well indeed.

The giant dahlias should be planted out first. These, because they are so large and tall, take a long time to grow and if you do not put them out early they may not be in flower until late in September. These huge exhibition varieties are naturally great favourites with growers who go in for showing and my advice to them is to plant early and if they live in the north then they must give protection to the plants with some form of glass covering until the end of the first week in June.

Hardening off

There are other factors that must be born in mind. Dahlia plants should never be put out in the open ground until they have been properly hardened off (see Chapter 3) Any gardener who, because of lack of frame space, has not been able to do the hardening as advised earlier, must delay planting for several days until the leaves and stems have hardened up. To put out soft plants is merely to court disaster.

Sodden and Dry Soil

Often there are soil problems to be faced, and this is especially true where gardeners have to cope with clay land. It is quite possible to have a very wet May, or even a wet May preceded by a wet April, and in this case the soil will be so sodden that it cannot be cultivated or planted up. The gardener is forced to defer the planting of his dahlias until the soil has dried out sufficiently. Should wet weather continue, and the gardener feel that the plants must go out because they are spoiling in their pots, then I suggest this method. First, arrange for some soil to be dried out. When the time for planting comes, place some planks on top of the soil, to walk on. Make holes in the wet ground and add some of the dried soil around the root ball of each plant. The wet soil can then be pressed around lightly.

Sometimes the soil can be so dry at planting time that it is necessary to pour plenty of water into the holes for the plants, besides watering well after planting and firming. Only in this way can dahlias be assured of a good start. It helps, too, if the plants growing in the pots are given a thorough watering early in the morning. Some gardeners stand the pots in a galvanised bath of water so that they really do get soaked through.

Gardeners who strike their own cuttings will have no difficulty in looking after them from the time they leave the greenhouse until the time they are planted in their flowering position. When the plants come from nurserymen, however, they may be so long in transit that the ball of soil around the roots is dry. In this case I advise plunging the plants in a bucket of water and leaving them for an hour or so before setting them up.

(By the way, the tops of the plants sometimes become broken off during a journey, and in this case, it is only possible to plant the roots and rely on a new stem developing later. In the case of really bad packing, or mishandling, it may be worth complaining and asking for a complete replacement. But with one or two damaged plants in a big order, one should just put in the roots and hope for the best.)

Situation

Although the gardener may have to put up with whatever soil his garden contains, he can certainly decide on the spot where the dahlias are to be grown. More important almost than soil is the situation, which must be an open one, so that the sun can reach all the plants. It is only in full sunlight that the dahlia can really do its best, though I have seen fair results in partial shade.

Shade only produces 'drawn plants' which are long and lanky, above their normal height. The flowers are robbed of their proper depth of colour and 'finish', and in the autumn they gradually become paler and even lose their pristine character. Choose a spot that is not too windswept, as the dahlia is apt to be damaged by gales. Provide some protection if there are prevailing winds. If you have to grow a plant in a somewhat exposed position, as so often happens in parks, then you must stake them earlier and more carefully. The ideal spot for dahlias is a gentle slope to the south, but one seldom finds this in the normal garden. Do not choose a steep slope or you will have trouble with watering.

Tuber Planting

Growers who prefer to plant tubers rather than struck cuttings will put these in the ground about the middle of April. The tubers, of course, are the old roots which are almost dormant and so the plants cannot be injured by frost until the shoots are actually through the ground. When the shoots do come through they are invariably much hardier and sturdier than those of struck cuttings, so they will stand up to a little frost without coming to any harm. If some shoots are through the ground by the middle of May and are then cut by a late frost, this will do very little harm to the plant; further shoots will soon appear.

The tubers should be planted 4in below the surface, in heavy clay soil, and as deep as 5in. below the surface in light sandy soil. (These distances are measured from the tops of the tubers.) Planting must be done firmly and with the tubers perpendicular. A little extra soil can be drawn up around the stems of the plants to protect the young shoots from frosts, and this is often done with dahlias whose shoots come through the ground early in May. At the end of May the soil can be hoed away from the plants again to leave the ground level.

I have found, when making trials, that tuber planting results in earlier flowering, on the whole, but that the plants themselves are never as vigorous or as tall, in the long run, as cuttings of the same varieties planted out about the same time and given exactly the same treatment.

Planting Distances

Different types of dahlias, naturally, need different amounts of space in which to grow. If the plants are being grown for a wonderful decorative effect one will aim to arrange them so that the soil is hidden and that nothing is seen but beautiful flowers and foliage. If, on the other hand, the aim is to provide the home with plenty of cut flowers then temporary paths may be left in between every three or four rows, to allow for ease of picking. Cut-flower rows, incidentally, usually run from north to south, and the plants are put out on a 2½ft square basis, with paths 2½ft wide. Further details about this method of culture will be found in Chapter 7.

Normally Decorative Dahlias and normal Cactus Dahlias need about 3–3½ft of room. Smaller Decoratives and Paeony-flowered Dahlias will be satisfied with 2½–3ft, as will Stars and Collarettes. Pompons and Charms, which grow to a height of about 2½ft, are often planted at intervals of 3ft one way and 2ft the other. Bedding dahlias, on the other hand, can easily be 18in apart.

It is impossible, however, to give hard and fast rules, because on poor sandy soils plants never grow so well as on nicely manured loams, and in a very dry season less growth will be produced than in a year when there is sufficient rain week by week. Also, much depends on how the plants are managed: if they are regularly and heavily disbudded, and the number of branches is deliberately restricted, then of course the individual dahlias need less room than when they are allowed to grow quite naturally. I have known experts grow the giant exhibition varieties as close as $2\frac{1}{2}$ feet square and by restricting the numbers of stems and blooms they have had wonderful results.

Nurserymen do try to indicate, in their catalogues the heights of their varieties, but these may easily vary by 6 to 8 in from one soil to another or from one district to another. So, although I like to think that the space required by a plant is always proportionate to its height, this certainly is not true. There are kinds which seem to spread out far more than others, and so the beginner must be prepared to give plants more room, in the first year, than they need. When he has discovered how the varieties behave on his own land and under his particular type of management, he should make notes that summer so that he will know exactly the distances to plant the following season.

It is usual to give more room to plants being grown for exhibition purposes than to similar varieties planted out in a border to make a brave show. In the case of the flowering border, the taller varieties will naturally be planted at the back and the shorter varieties in the front, with the medium-sized varieties in between. It is important not to allow the taller varieties to overshadow the shorter ones, and one needs to plan the border so that it faces the sun. Any particularly beautiful varieties could be planted at the ends of the border, where they would be seen to best advantage.

In such a border the plants should be set out in staggered rows. This is sometimes called the zig-zag method. When the front row has been planted, the dahlias in the second row will be positioned exactly mid-way between the dahlias in the front row, and in the third row the plants will be exactly behind those of the front row, and so on. In this way the plants get a better chance of showing themselves off.

Beginners are warned not to overcrowd a border, through over-enthusiasm. Anyone with common sense and a desire to succeed can take dahlia cuttings and split up tubers, so that after the first year the stock could easily have been increased by six. I would recommend starting with a few different varieties and from these making your choice as to the kinds or colours to be kept and propagated. The following year a few new varieties could be bought, to keep up the interest.

Some people like to plant out dahlias in a herbaceous border or even in a flowering shrub border, and there of course the plants can be given a little more room than usual; the distances already suggested will act as a guide. Five or six plants of one variety could be put in to form a bold group and fill a gap. These groups are often at the back of the border, and they do provide plenty of colour in midsummer when herbaceous borders tend to look drab. In the case of a shrub border dahlias are usually planted out in the early years, while the specimens are still growing to their full height and when, if dahlias were not used, the border might look rather bare.

The keen dahlia grower of many years standing will plan his special dahlia border in the winter, using squared paper, and so he will be ready by the month of May. This early planning enables him to propagate the number of different varieties he needs and to set them out at the right distance apart, and with no clashing of colours, such as puce pink next to bright red. He will know exactly the right distances to plot out for the various varieties, on his squared paper, because he will have kept a note-book during past summers and will have the heights and widths of each kind carefully recorded. A good gardener is not only a careful craftsman but an intelligent recorder as well.

Planting Out Pot-raised Plants

When you have prepared the plan and so know where each dahlia is going to be, it is a good idea to take a number of dwarf bamboos and push them into the soil exactly where the plants are to go. Some gardeners prefer to prepare large labels and push these in at the appropriate positions. This means, however, that a label is required for each dahlia instead of one good label for a group of dahlias of the same type and colour. For this reason I much prefer the bamboo method.

These bamboos, of course, will not be put out until the plot has been prepared as advised in the previous chapter, and the top $\frac{1}{2}$ in of soil well raked so that all the particles of soil are finer than a grain of wheat. The land must not be lumpy but 'friable', to use the gardener's term. It is unadvisable to plant out dahlias in heavy clay soils when the land is wet. It is better to keep the plants in their pots for a bit than to try to put them out into sodden land. Tramping about on such land is apt to make it set hard like cement, though this is less likely if planks are used to walk on.

Once the soil is in the right condition, i.e. not too wet or too dry, make a hole with a trowel that will take the ball of soil at the base of the plant without any difficulty. I always plant this ball an inch deeper than it was growing in the pot and this makes for ease of watering for the first week or so after planting. Do not attempt to break the ball of soil surrounding the roots, just remove the crock at the base of the ball and set it in the hole prepared by the trowel. Firm it in well, scrape some fine soil round the top of the plant and firm this also. Then, having made sure that the roots are really well bedded in, label the plant and if necessary provide it with a stake or bamboo to which it will be tied as it grows.

When it is feared that there may be trouble from winds, it is sensible to set out the dahlias a little closer than normal. A distance of $2\frac{1}{2}$ ft between one plant and another can be sufficient for any variety of dahlia, and when tall-growing varieties are put out as close as this the plants will protect one another. It is when dahlias are planted 4 to 5 ft apart that they are often battered, because each plant has to take the force of the gale.

Some gardeners take a bucketful or two of John Innes Compost,* so that they can fill this in right round the ball of soil as planting proceeds. They claim that this gives dahlias a better start. Whether this method is adopted or not, it is important to plant really firmly and to leave a little depression below the level of the normal soil around the stem of the dahlia. A fortnight or so later the hoeing between the plants will ensure that the soil is drawn towards the dahlias and thus the depressions are gradually filled in. Incidentally, if the soil is heavy, you will find it impossible to plant firmly if the ground is wet, which is another reason for delaying planting.

Dahlias can be harmed by overwatering just as much as by lack of moisture. Be careful, therefore, with the sticky heavier soils and never overwater them. It is much better to encourage roots to seek moisture for themselves than to give it to them continually and, so to speak, make them 'lazy'. Some gardeners claim for this reason that it is a mistake ever to put water into the hole at planting time. Instead they put the 'rain fan' into position for an hour or two and water the whole bed a few hours before planting.

Plants Sent from Nurseries

Not every gardener is in a position to raise his own plants, and in any case beginners may prefer to buy in plants. Plants sent from nurseries should arrive carefully packed by rail or by post. The nurserymen are not likely to send you plants until about the end of May when it is time to plant, but to save carriage they will

* Or 'Alex NO- SOIL' Compost

have to knock each ball of soil out of its pot. So the plants will come to you, as it is termed, ex-pots.

Do not remove the wrappers from the ball of soil until the moment of planting. When the plants arrive put them still in their wrappers in a bowl, with about an inch of water. Cut off the top part of the wrapping paper with a pair of scissors, to expose the leaves and stems and so prevent them from yellowing. The plants can be allowed to remain in their bowl of water for a day or so, and then, very carefully, the excess water can be poured off. It is a good idea to carry the plants still in their bowls to the bed where planting is to be done. The holes will be a little shallower than for plants grown at home because the balls of soil will have shrunk a little during transit and the soaking.

An alternative to putting the wrapped roots in water is to remove the paper straight away and pot up the dahlias into 4 in pots, using John Innes Potting Compost 2. The plants can be allowed to grow on in these pots for a week or two and then be planted out with a bigger ball of soil around the roots, with the minimum of disturbance. This potting-on method does of course mean that the gardener has to have somewhere to put the plants before he sets them out in the garden. It may be a frame, or a sheltered spot, or even a sunny courtyard. Whichever method is adopted, the purpose is to keep the plants 'happy' until they can grow in the spot that has been allotted to them.

Protection

Once the dahlias have been planted in their right positions, and you are absolutely certain that the varieties have been properly labelled, you must make sure that the small plants will be protected from cold winds. One method is to drive short stakes into the ground 4 ft apart and then tack some strips of old sacking to these, so making a temporary barrier against winds.

As one can easily have frosts up to the end of June, it may be necessary to protect the plants by covering them with sheets of newspapers at night-time. Since frosts only appear on calm still nights the newspaper will not be blown away when it is needed. Individual plants can be covered with Access frames, large glass jam jars, or even upturned flower-pots, the last two types of protection being removed during the day. Taking care over protection against frost always pays dividends.

If the weather should be very dry after planting, it may be necessary to do some overhead watering, but if so it should be done about 10 a.m., so that the plants have a chance of drying out by night time. Dry plants do not suffer from frosts as badly as wet ones.

Planting out Tubers

As mentioned, some gardeners prefer to plant tubers rather than plants produced from struck cuttings. It is necessary, of course, for the bed to be cultivated properly beforehand, at least to the depth of planting.

Look for the buds, or 'eyes' as they are called, on the tubers, and make sure that these are facing upward. The tubers can be laid horizontally or vertically, but make certain that it is resting firmly on the bottom of the hole. Experts disagree, in the case of plants, as to when stakes should be driven into the ground, but there is little disagreement in the case of tubers, for if you do not do the staking at planting time you can very easily drive a pointed stake through the tuber and ruin it if this work is done some weeks later.

It helps the tubers if a handful of the John Innes Compost 2 is put over and around them at planting time, before the rest of the soil is put back. There is no need to leave a space above the tuber, for watering should not be necessary. In fact it is not advisable to water tuber-planted dahlias for the first month or so. If the plants grow quickly there is a chance that some of the shoots may be through the soil by the middle or end of May. In this case it is a good idea to earth up these shoots to protect them, though even if one or two of them are ruined by frost, there is little doubt that further shoots will appear from down below.

'De Sarasate'

6 Managing Dahlias

Once the dahlias are in their beds and borders they must be kept growing steadily. This entails providing them with supports, protecting them from various enemies, and seeing that they are fed and watered correctly.

Weeding

Most gardeners, even if they are beginners, will realize the importance of keeping down weeds. This is comparatively easy to do if a sharpened Dutch hoe is used once a week, to cut through the top $\frac{1}{2}$ in. of soil and so leave a loose surface. This top $\frac{1}{2}$ in. of loose soil is sometimes called a dust mulch and it helps prevent the cracking of heavy soils in dry weather. Gardeners who hate hoeing will be glad to know that this work must cease late in July or early in August, for dahlias are surface rooters and the roots tend to come right up to the top of the soil at that time. This is the reason why mulching is so important, far more important in fact than watering. Naturally, as the plants grow and cover the ground, the shade they produce tends to discourage the growth of annual weeds.

The Importance of Mulching

One of the most valuable things I learned from Stuart Ogg, in my early years, was mulching. Many commercial growers of his calibre use well-rotted straw and stable manure, if possible, to spread over the soil to a depth of about 2 ins. Others who cannot get hold of horse or even cow manure use plain straw for the purpose, and over this apply a fish fertilizer with 10 per cent potash content at 2 or 3 oz to the square yard. Home-made compost, when this is fully rotted and ready, makes a first-class mulch. Do not be tempted to use lawn mowings because they are apt to heat up in dry weather and damage the plants. In wet weather they become a slimey mass, which is equally disagreeable. In any case, lawn mowings are full of weed seeds.

'Jimmy Meredith'

The use of fresh sawdust is also to be avoided. The sawdust is apt to have a denitrifying effect on the soil, that is to say, it causes the soil organisms to abandon doing their normal job of keeping the dahlias going and start trying to rot down the powdered wood.

My favourite mulch, which I use every year, is sedge peat. It is easily available, it contains no diseases, pests or weed seeds, and is much beloved by dahlias. Also, it improves the soil and the worms like it. The bed is thus left in a far better condition after dahlia growing than before.

A mulch should be applied during the latter half of July, although I do not mind doing it earlier than this. There seems no reason at all why sedge peat, for instance, should not be applied early in July or even late in June. A sedge peat mulch all over the ground to the depth of $\frac{1}{2}$in. is what is needed.

The Intelligent Use of Water

A good mulch not only smothers annual weeds but also, of course, acts as a barrier between the hot sun and the soil. It protects the soil from surface winds as well. Thus the moisture in the ground is kept there and not dissipated into the air. In many overseas countries where dahlias can be grown there are areas where it is so hot that even good mulching needs to be assisted by efficient watering, irrigation and perhaps shading too.

In this country, however, dahlias seldom feel the need of extra moisture until the beginning of August. One year, when the summer was particularly dry, my acreage of cut flower dahlias did not require watering at all until 20 August, because it had been mulched with straw a foot deep. When water has to be given it must be done in a big way. It is no good just giving dribs and drabs. A hose, with a square area sprinkler at the end of it, should be left in position for at least two hours. Watering can always be done through the sedge peat, through the straw or through whatever other type of mulching material has been used.

Watering with a sprinkler is much the best method. When the water is thrown into the air it is thoroughly aerated and so cannot damage the blooms of the plants, which is what happens, curiously enough, with water straight out of the tap. It is seldom necessary to give dahlias this artificial rain more than once every ten days, in the case of light sandy soils, and in the case of heavy clay land probably no more than once every three weeks. For some gardeners, who have perhaps just taken over a garden, a hose or a square area rainer is too great an expense.

The alternative, of course, is to use a watering can but each plant ought to be given about two canfuls. That is about four gallons. Applying large quantities of water like this takes a great deal of time, which is why few people do it, but to give less when the plants need it is just very foolish.

Newly planted dahlias need plenty of water

The bulk of the watering has to be done, as a rule, when the flower buds are first developing. The need for water continues as the flowering season gets to its peak, but beginners should realize (a) that dahlias can be grown without extra water being given, at any rate in heavy soils, if direct mulching is done, and (b) that it is quite possible, with clay soils, to overwater. All gardeners agree that watering is unnecessary from about the third week of September onwards.

Adding Further Plant Foods

When mulching is carried out with some form of strawy animal manure, or when it is done with plain straw or sedge peat plus fish manure, extra nourishment will be given in the right form and at the right time. When the rain comes plant foods will be washed down into the soil below, and when no rain appears artificial rain will have to be given instead, to achieve this. In my own garden, on heavy land, sedge peat and fish manure are the only extra feeds that the plants get. If, however, I had to cope with a dry sandy soil it would probably be necessary to use one of the liquid plant foods. These can be bought today in bottles or cans ready for dilution.

Dahlias do not need a great deal of nitrogen, and so one should look carefully at the formula on the container. The ideal type of liquid manure is one with a potash content as high as 10 per cent, phosphates as high as 6 to 8 per cent and the nitrogen as low as 4 per cent. If it was found impossible to obtain a liquid manure with a formula of this kind some extra potash in the form of wood ashes could be applied, at about ½ lb to the square yard. Extra feeds need not begin until the beginning of August and they should certainly cease by 15 September.

The advantage of using liquid plant foods is that they are taken up by dahlias within a day or two of their being applied. There are certain types of apparatus on the market which can be attached to trickle irrigators or hoses, so that as the water passes along the hose it picks up the exact quantities of liquid manure needed and feeds it to the plants automatically. These 'diluters', as they are called, have a dial at their head which can be set to ensure that a precise amount of liquid manure is automatically abstracted from the container, in accordance with the needs of the plants.

Do not assume, however, that the secret of good dahlia growing is feeding in the summer. It isn't. Far too many people ask me, when they see some magnificent blooms in a show, to tell them the name of the particular 'elixir' that has been used to produce such beauty. The proper answer would be a combination of experience, 'sweat', constant attention, high humus content in the soil, and what has not yet been mentioned, correct disbudding.

Stopping and Cutting Back

The expert chrysanthemum grower, Mr R. G. James, with whom I once worked, used to demonstrate very clearly the advantage of pinching out the growing points of chrysanthemum plants in order to force the side buds into growth. (These side buds are found at the base of the axels of the leaves.) Many of these buds will lie dormant quite happily until they discover that the main growing point of the plant on which they are situated has been removed. This is called 'timing', because by this means you could cause outdoor varieties of chrysanthemums to come into flower two or three weeks earlier than they would normally. The flowers would thus be ahead of their time.

After years of experience I discovered that this principle could be applied to dahlias. When dahlias are put out they consist of one only stem, and the gardener has to encourage the plants to send out a number of branches. If he waits until a flower bud appears at the top of the stem the check is then automatic, and the buds lower down break into growth without the plant being 'timed'. If you want earlier flowering in quantity you must pinch out the growing points a week or so after planting, and so cause this growing out of the base of the buds to take place earlier.

Some dahlia experts disdain 'timing' or 'stopping', preferring to practise 'cutting back'. They wait until the plant has produced eight pairs of true leaves and the stem is as thick as a man's little finger. They then take a sharp knife and cut the plant down severely to a point just above one of the buds lower down. Sometimes they are so severe in this cutting back that they remove five pairs of good leaves, though usually only three pairs of leaves are removed at this time. For beginners this is a frightening operation because what appears to be a strong growing plant is reduced to a small specimen.

The result of this hard cutting back, however, is that strong shoots develop at the base of the leaves. In about four weeks' time six good laterals or side stems may be produced, quite as strong as the original stem that was cut back. If only four of these are allowed to remain it will be found that strong branches like this flower profusely. The gardener must encourage dahlias to build up a strong frame to start with, because this strong frame, together with the leaves produced, will in turn build up a good root system. Hard cutting back, therefore, is an example of being cruel to be kind.

People who have small gardens and are anxious to have some very early blooms may, if they wish, allow a few of the plants to go unstopped. As a result the first main flower, or 'crutch bloom' as gardeners sometimes call it, will be produced. Sometimes the flower which develops from this centre bud will be coarse and poor, but in a number of varieties it will be quite satisfactory. So although one stops to get a quantity of earlier flowers and stronger plants, the dahlias can also be allowed to grow naturally.

It is possible to do this stopping when the plants are still in their pots, and some gardeners say that doing this prevents them from ever being pot-bound. I prefer, however, to wait until the plants have started to grow well in the border in which they are to flower. I start the work, as a rule, about the end of June and may not finish it until well on in July, for one variety does not grow as quickly or as strongly as another.

It is not necessary to carry out any stopping at all in the case of dwarf bedding dahlias, and often this is unnecessary also with smaller-sized free-flowering varieties of Cactus Dahlias. On the other hand it is probably correct to say that it is always necessary and advisable in the case of all larger-flowering kinds.

There is one further point to mention in connection with this pinching out of growing points, and this concerns plants grown from tubers. When the shoots appear above soil level it is important to leave only the strongest. The others should be cut back right to their base. The one remaining shoot should then develop similarly to the main shoot from a pot plant, and should be stopped or cut back in the usual way when it has produced eight pairs of good leaves. The only difference is that this will usually be about ten days or a fortnight before it is time to stop similar varieties raised from cuttings.

Staking and Supporting

Just as people vary enormously from each other, short and tall, strong and weak, so with dahlias. Some have wonderfully strong stems and never seem to need much support, others are always weak and their flowers droop and never seem able to look at you. Then there are varieties that are sometimes weak, sometimes strong and these are most annoying. They may, for instance, be strong in your friend's garden and weak in yours. I am amazed, as I travel to various parts of the world, to find that varieties which are weak-stemmed in my own garden in Arkley are strong-stemmed elsewhere, for example in the gardens of Claremont just outside Capetown. It isn't always a question of feeding, although of course if you give dahlias too much nitrogen they will become soft, and if you feed them with plenty of potash in the form of wood ashes they will be strong and firm.

Dahlias have succulent stems on the whole and do need some support. This does not mean that the gardener must use large high stakes that look unsightly all through the summer. Medium-sized varieties can be supported quite happily with small bamboos or prunings from apple trees, especially in the early stages. In the case of taller plants one good bamboo of the right height is usually enough, although in my own garden, for the huge Decoratives, I sometimes use three bamboos pushed into the ground at an angle of about 50 degrees so that they widen at the top and then the branches of the dahlias can be tied

Four-foot canes, set one foot deep in the plot make ideal supports for dahlia plants

in more naturally. It is only in the case of the very large Decorative types of dahlia planted in exposed situations, like those in parks, that tall green-painted wooden stakes are really necessary.

Galvanized stakes have the advantage of not rotting away, and also they are not bulky or unsightly. The snag, of course, is that they are rather expensive in the first place!

The plants can be tied with a variety of materials to the stakes. There is green twill twine, which is a very durable cotton product, or good raffia, or which I have used successfully lastex rubber yarn. This yarn has the great advantage that it gives as the stem of the plant grows and yet keeps it quite secure. Unfortunately it is not always available. Many gardeners prefer a type of soft string called fillis. One can buy 3– or 4–ply fillis, the former being a little cheaper than the latter, and stronger too. In most cases 3–ply fillis will be quite adequate. Flexible wire is another possibility, and can be used as shown in the illustration.

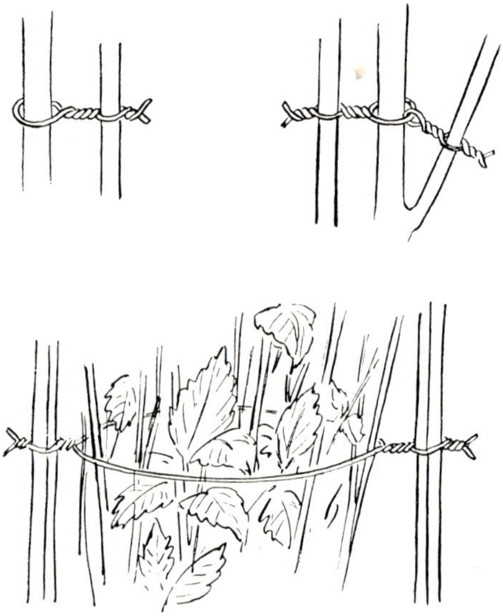

Methods of tying up using flexible wire

The three main points to remember when staking are: (1) use a strong enough stake which will not snap off in a gale, and see that its base is driven well into the ground, about 12 in. deep; (2) see that the stakes are not obvious, so that the appearance of the border is not spoilt, and (3) never tie the stems very tightly to the stakes and bamboos, because when the stems grow the string will cut into them.

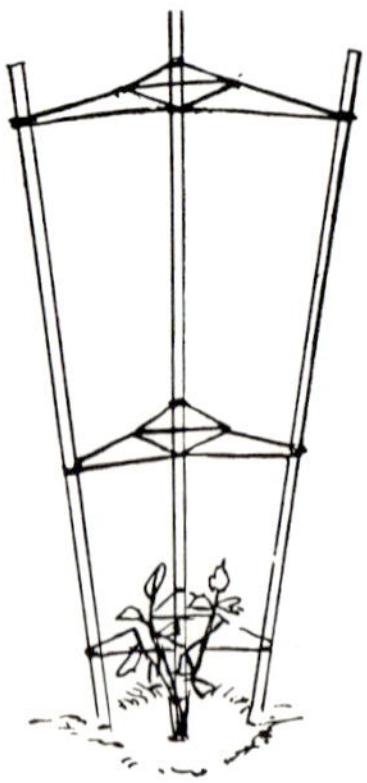

Make a framework of string and let the shoots find their own support

When wooden stakes or bamboos are to be used it is essential to stand them first in a bucketful of Rentokil preservative for at least three hours, to prevent them from rotting in the ground. Never use a stake that will appear a foot or so above the top of the plant when it is fully grown. This means having a variety of stakes available. See that the stakes are put in early so that, as the plants grow, the branches may be tied in as desired. When three stakes are used at least two lengths of green twine or raffia may be used to encircle them, one at a height of 2 ft, and the next a foot above.

Another reason why staking is done is that during a rainy season the amount of water held by a large bloom is considerable. This may easily cause the stem to crack or bend. Gardeners who like to grow immense blooms often find it necessary to provide canes for individual blooms and stems to make certain that they cannot be damaged by wind or rain. There is no need to use the thickest bamboo canes for this purpose, and in any case the thinner types are cheaper and not so obvious. They provide just the type of support needed by the stems.

There is no need to provide bamboos for the normal bedding dahlia. The plants do not grow any higher than 18 in. or so, and being planted quite close together they can protect one another. Even dahlias growing as tall as 3 ft will not need a great deal of support and, in fact, I have often used pea sticks for such types of dahlias. The sticks are pushed in among the plants, so that as the leaves grow they will hide the brushwood completely.

Unfortunately, it is not always possible to guarantee that plants will keep to the heights mentioned in a book of this kind, or even in a reliable catalogue. After the first year, therefore, make certain you record how high each variety has grown in your garden and then the following season provide supports of the right height.

There are some very large, strong varieties of dahlias which need powerful support because they grow so tall and because they are so top-heavy. These varieties call for hard wood stakes 1 in. square and about 6 ft long. These, when they have been soaked in Rentokil Preservative, must be driven into the soil 18 in. down with a large wooden mallet or beadle, for they never stay firm when pushed in by hand. Trying to grow a huge top-heavy variety without an extraordinarily strong stake is just asking for trouble.

Stem Thinning

Many gardeners think it is vitally important to thin out the stems of dahlias. They tell you, for instance, that with Large Decoratives you should only leave about six or seven stems, and that growers who are going in for show blooms must reduce that number to four. With Medium Decoratives, on the other hand, it is suggested that you should have not more than ten stems, in the normal way, though if you propose to win prizes only six or seven stems should be allowed. With the Cactus and Semi-Cactus types the recommended numbers are ten and five.

These arbitrary instructions, which I was given as a young

man when I first started to grow dahlias, should only be used as a guide. The dahlia grower must consider the peculiarities of the varieties he is growing, and give individual attention and treatment. Restricting the number of branches too severely often results in coarseness and this is a disagreeable trait in any dahlia. If one finds that the blooms are in fact rather coarse the simple remedy is to leave a greater number of branches next year.

To a certain extent, the decision about the number of branches to be retained must depend on the soil and on the type of manuring carried out. More branches can be allowed on well fed heavy soils than on poorly fed sandy loams. Generally speaking, in this country, I find that successful growers rely on about six branches per plant with almost any variety they are growing for show. This number of branches, they say, gives them the desired size of bloom and the necessary strength of stem and yet prevents any hint of coarseness.

This reduction to five or six branches is made, of course, in the early stages, for no dahlia plant remains static after the first few branches have flowered and new growths must be allowed to take their place. The grower who cuts his flowers regularly, to have them in the house, ensures that more and more blooms will be produced as the year proceeds. Even when growing dahlias in flower borders and perhaps having no need for cut blooms, he should always remove the dead heads week by week, and cut back the stems at the same time.

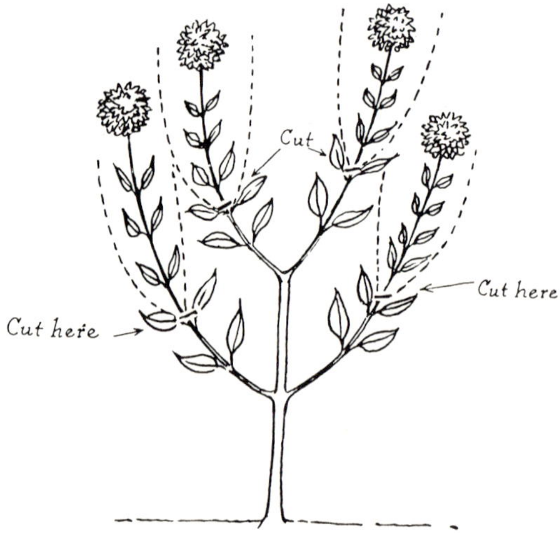

Diagram showing where to cut flowers so as to have a continuous display. Dotted lines show secondary growth

The whole question of stem thinning, or de-branching as some people call it, is bound up with exhibiting in the show beds. It is really only relevant when dahlias are being grown for show, and it is seldom necessary to carry it out if you are just growing for a grand garden display or even for cut flowers for the house.

Most people advise cutting the stem back quite hard, i.e. to the second pair of leaves from the base of the branch. It is in this way that new strong branches are encouraged. If you dislike overcrowded plants you can always do a certain amount of thinning, to let in light and air. Do not, however, thin out dahlias in this way unless you are really forced to. Remember that if you cut your flowers regularly you will have less time to wait for the second crop of blooms, and that your earlier flowering will not be adversely affected if, by cutting back hard, you encourage the new shoots to start to develop before some of the later first blooms have started to open.

Disbudding

The gardener who is growing dahlias for fun, to produce a glorious display, will not need to bother at all about disbudding. He carries out the initial stopping or timing, but after that allows the branches to grow and flower naturally. All he has to do is to see to the regular removal of dead blooms and the stems on which they were produced. If, however, he is keen on showing, or simply wants to produce larger blooms to brighten his garden or house, then he will embark on disbudding.

Disbudding is a very simple operation indeed. At the top of each flowering stem will be found three flower buds, one in the centre, one on either side. It is invariably the centre bud that is

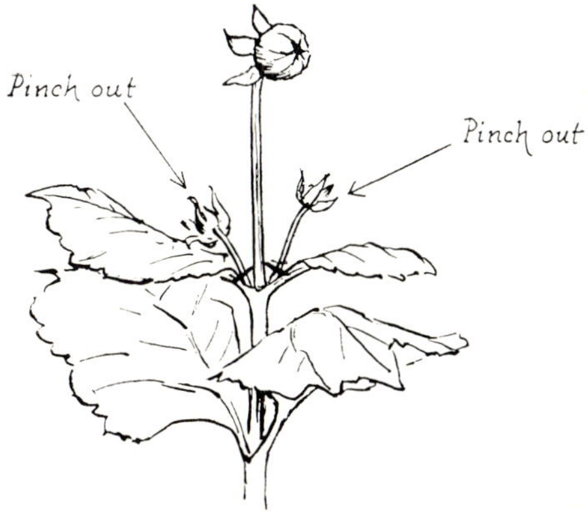

Disbudding a dahlia

the largest and tallest, and so this is left in position while the two side buds are pinched out. As the result of removing the two side buds, the centre flower grows larger and finer, while at the same time the stem tends to elongate.

Remove the side shoots as soon as possible after they are formed, and then there will be no difficulty in removing them with the sharp nail of the thumb and the forefinger. Most people prefer using the sharp blade of a knife to nick out the side shoots cleanly. Do not be afraid that this disbudding will necessarily reduce the number of large blooms per plant. With a large Decorative Dahlia I have had sixty good blooms or more a year, even when disbudding has been done rigorously.

In addition to this disbudding it is advisable to remove the side shoots emanating from the axels of the next two pairs of leaves. By preventing these side growths from developing you concentrate the sap into the bloom above and so obtain some very fine specimens. Don't bother about disbudding varieties of dahlias that are naturally small; the size of the flowers will hardly be improved by such methods. It is not necessary, for instance, to disbud the bedding varieties or the Charm varieties.

Although it is normally the centre flower bud that is retained when disbudding, one of the side buds could be selected if the central bud has been nibbled by a caterpillar or damaged by an earwig. Some exhibitors even say that by choosing a side bud rather than the centre bud you always get a longer and better stem in the end.

It is generally the large-flowered varieties that need rigorous disbudding. Varieties with medium-sized flowers can be disbudded just a little, here and there, but those that produce only small flowers need no disbudding at all, unless the gardener is anxious to increase the length of the stem. In this case he will disbud by taking out the centre bud and one of the side buds.

Retaining a side bud rather than the centre one may delay the time of flowering by as much as ten days, and therefore a gardener who is keen on spreading the flowering period of his dahlias over a longer time than usual can (a) leave all flowering buds on some branches, (b) disbud some other branches leaving the centre bud in position, and (c) carefully disbud the remaining branches by pinching out the centre bud.

7 Dahlias as Cut Flowers

Years ago the dahlia as a cut flower was much more popular on the Continent than it was in this country, but I think this was chiefly because we had not then learned to grow the right varieties. The qualities desired for a good cut flower are: (a) bright colour, (b) a nice long stem, and (c) the ability to last well in water when cut. The modern dahlia can fulfil all these conditions, but one must be careful to choose the right varieties.

The taller types are the most suitable for cut flower work, and nowadays hundreds and hundreds of boxes of dahlias find their way to flower markets, in this country, during the summer season. Years ago I was among those who first encouraged the planting of dahlias for the cut flower trade. I carried out trials on the lasting properties of cut dahlia blooms and, as the result of my experiments, was able to show that the period that dahlias will last in water often varies with the average temperature during a particular week. For instance, 'Crimson Flag', a popular cut flower, may easily last seven and a half days in water if the average temperature of the room is about 46 degrees F, but if the temperature rises to 60 degrees F the flower will probably last only five days.

If you go in for growing dahlias as a cut flower, you should aim to keep the different varieties in separate beds. The taller types may need to be at least $2\frac{1}{2}$ft apart, though with some of the Pompons 2ft is quite sufficient. The beds should be no wider than 5ft, preferably only 4ft, and there should be temporary pathways between them about 2ft wide. In this way all the flowers can be picked easily and no one has to walk on the beds themselves and disturb the plants.

The site for growing dahlias as cut flowers should be an open one, for to produce the heaviest crop and the best blooms one must avoid shade. On the other hand it is very good to choose a sheltered situation, because the plants are easily damaged by strong winds. For this reason I often put up temporary barriers of hessian nailed to strong posts driven into the ground 8ft apart. These posts are 3 in. across and 8 ft long, and being of chestnut they last a long time. They are driven 2 ft into the ground, at a distance of 4 ft away from the cut-flower section and on the side from which the prevailing wind comes.

Having chosen the area for the bed prepare the soil in accordance with the instructions given in Chapter 4. The management of dahlias grown as cut flowers differs very little from what I have described earlier, but about the middle of July I cover the soil with a layer of straw about 9 in. deep. This is put over the temporary paths as well as the rows where the dahlias are growing. The mulching smothers the annual weeds and helps keep the moisture in the ground; in a wet year the straw carpet makes the temporary paths quite pleasant to walk on.

If the cut-flower area is fairly large, the surface soil can be worked down to a fine tilth with a rotary cultivator towards the end of May. At the same time medium grade sedge peat is added at about half a bucketful to the square yard and a fish manure with a 10 per cent potash content at about 4 oz to the square yard. With a smaller area the land is just raked down level, the sedge peat and fish manure being added at the same time.

The cut-flower grower seldom finds it necessary or advisable to give further feeds of fertilizers during the summer. The exception is when the soil is sandy and the summer very dry. Then, of course, it is necessary to irrigate with an overhead sprinkler, and a good liquid manure, high in potash, can be used in addition.

The gardener who is keen on growing dahlias as cut flowers will propagate them as described in Chapter 3. The commercial grower, on the other hand, usually gets his tubers out of store and starts them into growth in the greenhouse at the beginning of February, or even as late as the middle of February. He often uses potato chitting trays for this purpose, first putting a 1-in. layer of sedge peat in the bottom. He sits the tubers on this and then covers them with just enough light soil or sedge peat to imbed them. His aim is to obtain about five good cuttings per tuber. These are struck around the edge of a 3-in. pot filled with sharp river silver sand or Vermiculite. He reckons to have the cuttings rooted in twelve to twenty days and he then pots them up individually into 3-in. pots, growing them on first of all in a cool greenhouse and later hardening them off in the frame. The cut-flower grower seldom pots up his dahlias from 3-in. to 5-in. pots, he just hasn't the time or the labour.

For some reason or other the date usually aimed at for planting out of doors is 21 May in the south, and 7 June in most parts of the north. The dahlias should be planted very firmly and, on the whole, a little deeper than normal. They should be $2\frac{1}{2}$ft apart and in straight lines, with about 2ft between the rows. The plants are best arranged in zigzag fashion, so that a dahlia in one row is not opposite another dahlia in the next.

It will then be necessary to arrange support. Strong chestnut posts are required, driven into the ground at the corners of the bed. At a height of about 3ft a crossbar should be nailed from post to post. It is from this crossbar that wires are stretched tightly from one end of the bed to the other, so that they run exactly between the dahlia rows. If, as normally happens, there are three rows of dahlias, then four parallel wires are needed, two running outside the bed and two stretched tightly in between the dahlia rows. Binder twine, tied between these four wires at intervals, is used to provide squares through which the dahlias will grow quite naturally. If tall varieties are being grown, a second crossbar should be nailed on a foot higher, with wires attached in the same way, and binder twine tied across.

I find that old government telephone wire is suitable for this purpose. It is strong, flexible, steel-stranded and waterproof-covered. It can be bought in several thicknesses. The whole idea of this system of wires and string is to save the individual tying-up of plants. The branches grow through the 'squares' provided by the wires and string, and no accurate tying-up has to be done at all.

If the planting is done on 21 May it should be possible, about the beginning of June, to stop each plant by cutting out the main stem. Of the side growths that result eight to ten will be selected, and this usually means that, about the end of July, the first lot of disbudding will have to take place. After all, the cut-flower grower aims at getting his blooms ready to use in the house, or ready to sell, a fortnight or so before his neighbour.

If all goes well, the plants should be perfectly happy, growing in their straw mulch bed. The flowers should be cut just before they reach perfection, and to get them at the right moment it will be necessary to go over the plants twice a week. If flowers are produced in abundance, as they so often are, the excess should be cut at the same time and either given away or put on the compost heap to rot down for manure. It is most important never to allow any of the blooms to fade or go to seed.

Cut the dahlias with stalks as long as possible so that they look their best in vases. This sometimes means that it is necessary to remove other flowers still in bud on a lower part of the stem. The moment the flowers have been cut they should be placed in deep water, and before they are used in the house it is a good thing to dip the bottom 3 in. of the stem in a bucket of boiling water, for ten seconds. This greatly improves the keeping quality of the flowers. When the stems are taken out of the boiling water, they should be placed in a bucket or bath full of cold water for five or six hours. The water should rise, as gardeners say, 'right up to the necks' of the stems, so that they are firmly gorged with moisture before being displayed in vases in the house.

As will be seen from the following chapter, it is possible to grow dahlias as cut flowers in the greenhouse. Then, of course, blooms may be cut in June onwards, until flowers are available outside. At this point I advise cutting the plants down to within 6 in. of soil level and letting them grow up again. They will start to flower profusely towards the end of September and go on blooming through the month of October. Thus you get two crops a year from dahlias planted out in a greenhouse, and the flowers come in at a time when outdoor growers do not have them available. There are some years when this scheme is not particularly profitable, for instance, when there are no late

'Twiggy', a silvery-pink water-lily-form dahlia that makes a fine cut flower subject in any garden

frosts in September or October, and so flowers are cut and sold right the way through to the beginning of November. Perhaps there is no cut-flower plant that gives such a constant, heavy yield of flowers as the dahlia, and which will go on blooming quite happily for so long a period.

Varieties

Lists of the great majority of dahlias available today will be found in Chapters 11, 12, 13, 14 and 15. Most of the Small Decoratives, Miniature Decoratives and Pompons can be used as cut flowers, as well as certain varieties from other groups. In this chapter I am listing only the varieties I have grown myself or seen grown for the cut-flower trade, and which I know from experience would be suitable. Please, therefore, regard this list as only a guide and do not be afraid to try out new varieties as they appear, or launch out with other varieties if they seem suitable.

DECORATIVES

Amber Lights	– light bronze, prolific and early
Amethyst	– excellent for cutting, the nearest to blue – a lavender
Angora	– attractive, white, fimbriated (split petal ends)
Annie Gray	– pale yellow, excellent form very near pompon
Biddenham Beauty	– flame red, form near that of the water-lily
Black Beauty	– deepest red, early
Blossom	– attractive pastel pink, very formal
Buttersweet	– deep yellow with plenty of bloom
Chinese Lantern	– orange and gold, an eye-catching beauty
David Howard	– deep orange with contrasting copper foliage
Dedham	– long-stemmed lilac and white blend, delightful
Director	– scarlet, fimbriated
Dr Grainger	– strong-stemmed, bright orange, a famous dahlia
Edinburgh	– a great favourite, purple-tipped white
Flutterby	– water-lily form, scarlet and yellow
Gerrie Hoek	– pink water-lily dahlia, still a great favourite
Glorie V. Heemstede	– one of the famous water-lily dahlias, pale yellow

Hamari Fiesta	– red and gold blends, most attractive
Happy Birthday	– deep blood red, a consistent variety
Horn of Plenty	– raised in Holland, a flame of perfect form
Iver's Choice	– bright red, excellent for garden use
Lady Tweedsmuir	– from Scotland, lavender, on good stems
Larkford	– masses of bloom, lavender pink
Mary Richards	– another famous British dahlia, blends of pink and white
Orchid Lilac	– a northern-raised beauty
Requiem	– a deep purple
Rothesay Robin	– a formal deep pink, one of the best
Schwieter's Kokarde	– orange, on long stems
Swiss Miss	– pink tipped white, most appealing
Tinker's White	– one of the best cut-flower whites
Trendy	– another newcomer, scarlet and yellow blends, beautiful
Twiggy	– pink water-lily, everyone's favourite
Vicky Crutchfield	– neat shell-pink with good stem for cutting

CACTUS (C) AND SEMI-CACTUS (SC)

Alvas Doris (C)	– bright spiky red from New Zealand
Black Flash (SC)	– deepest red on good stems
Brigadoon (C)	– mid-red, very prolific
Cheerio (SC)	– cheery red-tipped silver, very popular
Daydream (SC)	– pink and white, small and sparkling
Doris Day (C)	– best small red, from Holland
Hoek's Yellow (SC)	– a famous cutting flower from Holland, widely grown
Klanstad Kerkrade (C)	– palest yellow with mauve nuance, one of the best since the War
Lilac Veil (SC)	– strong stems, plenty of bloom all season
Mick (C)	– lilac blends, a British-raised cutting flower
Orange Nymph (C)	– fimbriated petals add to the attraction of this Dutch flower
Pwll Coch (SC)	– a good red from Wales, (the name means 'pool of fire')
Richard Marc (C)	– pastel pink and yellow, very attractive
Seren Da (SC)	– an unusual lemon and mauve blend, (the name means 'Good Star')

Starfire (C)	– scarlet and salmon, wiry blooms on strong stems
Tradition (C)	– a Dutch beauty, pure salmon-pink
White Swallow (SG)	– a very good white for all purposes
Worton Blue Streak (SC)	– a good one for floral art, bright mauve

BALL

Amusing	– blends of scarlet and gold
Bubbles	– white and mauve on long stems
Chic	– royal purple, finishes like a tennis ball
Connoisseur's Choice	– bright red, one of the very best
Opal	– a very popular pink and white variety from Australia
Vaguely Noble	– deep purple, a recent arrival

POMPON

Andrew Lockwood	– lavender, petite
Glen Afton	– rich purple, lighter reverse petal
Jacky Brooks	– blends of gold, bronze and red
Little Conn	– a famous pom, bright red
Moor Place	– one of the best poms ever raised, maroon purple
Rhondda	– pink and white blends, perfect form
Willo's Night	– almost black, from Australia

In addition to these there is an attractive unusual variety which is usually included under the heading of bedders or double dwarf bedders. I refer to 'Bishop of Llandaff', which produces crimson-scarlet flowers and normally grows to a height of $2\frac{1}{2}$ ft. Its foliage is very dark, almost black in fact, and this makes it very useful for flower arranging.

8 Dahlias in the Greenhouse

The dahlia is not normally considered a greenhouse plant. Although, as is described in Chapter 3, most of the propagation of dahlias is of course done in the greenhouse, the plants themselves are grown out of doors. There are, nevertheless, two main advantages of growing dahlias in the greenhouse. One, of course, is that you can get the plants into flower early, and the other is that you can have them in flower very late in the year, long after the outdoor varieties have been cut down by the frost. There may be some particular reason for the amateur to want these advantages. Some blooms may be needed to enter at some flower arrangement competition, or certain varieties of dahlias may be required for, say, a birthday or a wedding anniversary. It is probably a good thing, therefore, to know something about growing dahlias in the greenhouse, even though you may not be considering selling the blooms for profit.

Those who go regularly to the Royal Horticultural Society's Show at Chelsea will know what wonderful exhibits, of almost all kinds of dahlias, are put up year after year. In order to be cut and arranged during the third or fourth week of May, the flowers need to be grown in greenhouses.

If the need arose, and if it were possible to install modern forms of lighting and heating, one should be possible to produce dahlias under glass that would flower almost all the year round. In our glasshouses at The Horticultural Training College at Arkley we had special Philips lamps which gave artificial sunlight. The use of special lamps for long periods would, of course, be expensive, and I have only tried to expand the flowering period, so that it lasts from May to the middle of November. In most years this has been quite successful.

The 'Dry Season'

In their natural habitat, dahlias start to grow when the rainy season comes and go on growing and flowering until the start of the dry season, when they die down. Thus year after year, in places like Mexico, dahlias spring up, flower for as long as possible and then, so to speak, 'pass out' until the tubers feel the presence of the natural moisture once more. This natural pattern should be taken as a guide by the greenhouse dahlia grower.

If you want to have early dahlias, either for show purposes or as cut flowers, you may like to try the following scheme. Pot up some tubers into 6-in. pots in, say, April. Then allow the plants to grow and flower in these during the summer. The pots should be stood in some sheltered but sunny spot, and watered regularly. Some people 'sink' the pots up to their rims in sand or sedge peat, with the result that a minimum of watering has to be done during the hot summer months. When it comes to the middle of September, gradually withhold the water so that you provide what might be termed an artificial dry period. The dahlia plants must be encouraged to start their 'resting period' early for early flowering the following season, so the sooner this resting period can start, the better.

Once the plants have died down and all the plant food has been passed back from the leaves into the tubers, these tubers may be stored in a dry frost-proof shed. The elaborated sap is manufactured in the leaves and stored in the tubers as 'starch', with the result that the plants have plenty to feed on when they make a start next season. We now have all the tubers on each individual plant clustered together within the ball of each pot. These are what are called 'pot tubers' for obvious reasons.

Potting Up Tubers

If these pot tubers are stored properly, so that they cannot be killed by the frost or rotted by too much moisture, they should then be in a nice firm, plump condition the following January. Then is the time to pot them up just as they are into 3-in. pots filled with John Innes Potting Compost 2.* It may be thought peculiar that the tubers that have been knocked out of a 6-in. pot should be able to fit into a 3-in. pot, but it must be remembered that all the soil is carefully removed from around the tubers when they are put into the storehouse for the winter, so there is little difficulty in getting the tubers to fit into a 3-in. pot the following January. If by chance the group of tubers is rather large, one of them may be cut away with a sharp knife so that the 'bunch' of small tubers will fit quite easily into the 3-in. pot.

Wash the pots well so that they are absolutely clean, then get

* Or Alex NO-SOIL Compost

one or two pieces of broken pot ('crocks') and place these concave side downwards over the drainage hole of each pot. It is most important to ensure that the excess moisture runs away, and so the crocks are there to prevent the hole at the base of the pot from becoming blocked. Do the potting really firmly, allowing the compost to trickle in between the tubers and then using a thin potting stick to firm in the soil. See that the pot is filled up with compost to within ½ in. of its rim.

When all the tubers have been correctly potted up into their separate pots, stand them on the staging of the greenhouse. The temperature of the house should be 55 degrees F at night time, and allowed to rise to 65 degrees F during the day. Never try and force the plants, just get them into growth quite naturally. The compost itself, of course, should be just moist when used for potting up, and should be kept like this afterwards. If the soil becomes too wet the tubers may rot. Only carry out regular watering, therefore, when growth becomes active. If you do this you should see some nice dahlia shoots appearing by the beginning of February.

Dis-shooting

We now come to the important matter of dis-shooting. Select the strongest shoot, which is usually the central shoot, and then carefully pinch out, or better still 'rub out', the other shoots. Gardeners use the term 'rubbing out' when the shoots are quite small and can therefore be removed by passing the thumb over the tuber to rub off the shoot. Allow about a fortnight for the plant to get over this 'operation', and then it should be possible to do the first potting on. This means transferring the ball of soil from the 3-in. pot into a 6-in. pot, and for this purpose John Innes Potting Compost 3 is used.

Into the 6-in. Pot

We must now turn to the preparation of the 6-in. pot. This must first be washed and allowed to dry. Three good crocks should then be placed in the bottom of the pot, concave shape downwards, and over this should be put an inch or two of John Innes Compost 3 so that when the ball of soil from the 3-in. pot is put in on top it is ½ in. from the rim of the new pot in which it is going to grow. Of course the compost in the base of the pot must be firm before the ball of soil is put in and the rough measuring done.

Take the smaller pot containing the tubers, place two fingers over the soil, one either side of the shoot, and turn the pot upside down. If you give the rim of the pot a slight tap on the bench the ball of soil should come out quite easily. All you have to do is to remove the two crocks at the bottom of this ball so that it can be transferred into the centre of the larger pot.

Whenever plants are potted on, the gardener must remember that it is tremendously important to see that the compost placed round the original ball of soil is just as firm, if not firmer, than the ball of soil itself. If the soil around the ball is loose the water given at watering time runs down the sides in the loose area and so never moistens the central ball. This is the reason that so many plants die after they have been potted on into a larger pot by a beginner. Use the potting stick that I have already mentioned and see that the new compost is really firm.

Potting Up Large Varieties

Of course, if you are going to try and grow very large varieties like the Giant Decoratives whose flowers are over 10 in. in diameter, then it is better to pot up at this stage into 10-in. or 12-in. pots. Some people advise potting on these Large Decoratives into 6-in. pots first and then later potting on once more into the larger sizes, but I reckon this to be a waste of time and energy.

Some readers may say that they do not want to go to the expense of buying large pots. In this case I advise the use of large boxes instead, for they are just as useful for the purpose. They should be treated first of all with Rentokil preservative, so that they really do last. If preferred, the insides of the boxes may be charred with a blow-lamp. Drainage holes must then be bored in the bottom of the boxes, which can easily be done with a red-hot poker if you do not have a brace and bit. The great thing is to give the dahlia a good root run, which will save a tremendous amount of watering and to a certain extent the necessity for extra feeding as well. One should aim at not having to give feeds at all until the plants are growing well and are even in their flowering quarters.

Feeding

The great advantage of using John Innes Compost is that it contains the plant foods needed by dahlias in the early stages and so helps to ensure that a good root system is built up. Once the stems are 18 in. high or more, especially if the plants are only growing in 6-in. pots, one can start to feed the plants every fortnight. There is far less room in a 6-in. pot than in a large box, and dahlias growing in a restricted condition will need some liquid manure.

The ideal feed to use is one of the liquid plant foods derived largely from organic sources like seaweed. It is available in a bottle, and should be diluted according to the instructions given on the label. The feed should be one that is properly balanced: the dahlia grower will not want to apply too much nitrogen and so send his plants all to leaf, but will need to use ample phosphates and potash.

There is a liquid feed known as 'Bio Plant Food' which I find gives good results. It can be used at the rate of 1 teaspoonful to a gallon of water for young plants, and 1 tablespoonful to a gallon of water for mature specimens. Each plant will probably need a quart of this dilute feed, once a fortnight at first, and then once a week when the flower buds start to appear.

Staking

The taller dahlias, of course, will need some staking and tying, just as they do out of doors, but obviously the stakes need not be as strong since the greenhouse provides protection from winds. The best type of greenhouse for dahlias is one where the glass goes well down to the ground, so that the plants get the maximum amount of light. Under such conditions the pots may be stood at floor level. If, on the other hand, the greenhouse has a side wall the dahlias must be spaced out well on the staging. In this case take care to see that they have sufficient head room. The best dahlias under glass are invariably grown in tall airy houses, which provide almost out-of-door conditions, plus the extra warmth and protection.

Dutch Lights

I grow my dahlias under glass in what are called Dutchlight Houses. These are greenhouses composed entirely of Dutch Lights, which are really large panes of glass with wooden frames to them. They are used by market gardeners for growing lettuces, melons, cucumbers and the like in frames. A Dutch Light consists of a single pane of horticultural glass (21 oz) which measures 56 in. by 28¾ in. This large frame is held in a wooden frame which has top and bottom rails 2½ in. by 1½ in. and sides consisting of wooden batons 2 in. by 2 in. with grooves into which the big sheet of glass can be slipped. A wooden stop is provided on the bottom rail to prevent the glass slipping down any further and another wooden stop is nailed onto the top rail to keep everything tight and shipshape.

When made up the frame should be 59 in. long and $31\frac{3}{4}$ in. wide. The groove into which the glass slips is cut into the side rails or batons $\frac{1}{2}$ in. deep and $\frac{1}{4}$ in. wide, and at a point $1\frac{1}{2}$ in. up the rail on one side only. Sometimes common deal is used, treated with a preservative like Rentokil, and also Western Red Cedar, but then the frames are dear. These glass lights form the sides of the house and similar Dutch Lights are used to form the roof. The glasshouse is therefore very simple in construction, and fairly inexpensive. Its main advantage is that it provides the dahlias with the maximum amount of light and head room.

Using the Greenhouse Border

The alternative to growing dahlias in pots or boxes, in the greenhouse, is to grow them in the greenhouse border. This border is prepared in exactly the same way as advised for dahlias growing out of doors (see Chapter 4). When the necessary dis-shooting has been carried out the dahlias can be planted out in exactly the same way as they would be planted out of doors. Usually, however, the soil is much drier because of the glass roof, so that a fair amount of watering may be necessary. Most growers plant their dahlias a little closer in greenhouse borders than they do in the open, if they are only going to use the plants for flower production in May and June. On the other hand, if they are hoping to cut the plants down late in June, in order to encourage a second flowering period from late September, then the planting distances advised for outdoor work should be followed rigorously.

Growers who want to save their tubers dig them up about the middle of July, with as much soil around their roots as possible, and plant them in big holes out of doors. Here the plants go on growing until the leaves die down naturally or until the plants are cut down by the frosts. Of course this removal of dahlias in July is only necessary if the house is needed for another crop, for instance, tomatoes. When a second crop of flowers is hoped for the tubers remain in the greenhouse until about November, when they are usually dug up and put on the compost heap to rot down and form manure.

When dahlias are planted in the greenhouse border, it is unusual for them to need feeding. Generally speaking they are very happy in the well-prepared soil, and because of the warmth and protection they receive they tend to grow almost too tall and too wide; in fact, they can make a nuisance of themselves. When choosing dahlias to grow in the greenhouse border, therefore, I usually concentrate on the Pompon varieties and particularly the smaller-flowered types. The taller, larger varieties are perhaps best grown with the pot or box system, for by this method the roots are somewhat restricted.

Hygiene is very important with dahlias to avoid virus infection. Use a good organic insecticide in the greenhouse

Pests and Diseases

Dahlias growing under glass are unfortunately subject to the same pests and diseases as are those growing in the open. In fact these attacks can be quite persistent because the plants tend to be softer and more succulent. On the other hand, it is much easier to control insect pests and fungus diseases in a greenhouse, with modern forms of fumigation, than out of doors. Aerosols and smoke bombs to use under glass can easily be bought from horticultural chemists.

9 Dahlias as Bedding Plants

For years the geranium held pride of place as the favourite main bedding plant. Our grandparents revelled in the good old-fashioned red, white and blue display which was produced throughout the summer by the 'Paul Crampel' Geranium or the almost royal 'Gustav Emich', together with blue lobelia and white alyssum. After a heavy rainfall 'Paul Crampel' is apt to look a little bedraggled, but 'Gustav Emich' always stands strong and firm and looks brilliant. To keep white alyssum flowering over a long period it is necessary to sprinkle a few seeds around the plants when bedding them out and then, when the original plants cease to flower, the little seedlings come up and start to bloom, so that you get a brave show for many more months of the year.

In the early days of King George V the red salvia, and particularly 'Harbinger', sprang into popularity. It was simple to produce and it went on flowering for a very long period. It was not long, however, before this in turn was ousted by the Dwarf Dahlia, and particularly by one of the varieties of Coltness Gem which proved to be the ideal bedding plant almost all over the country.

Today there are very large numbers of bedding varieties of the Coltness Gem type, and of other types too, for that matter. Some notable ones are 'Rita', an orange-scarlet cactus type, 'Jessie Ross', rose-pink, 'Mrs Stappers', crimson with bronze foliage, 'Rothesay Ruby', ruby-red, and 'Rothesay Castle', cream overlaid with rose. All bedding varieties go on flowering for weeks at a time, and require little or no attention. They grow no taller than 18 in. and can be planted out with success about 18 in. apart. Those that grow only 1 ft high can be planted as closely as 1 ft apart, thus making a regular mat of growth and smothering the weeds.

Planning Designs

It is possible, of course, to plan out various designs using dahlias only. You could have, for example, a large block of red dahlias in the centre and a surrounding edging of yellow Dwarf Dahlias, or white dahlias in the middle and red dahlias all around. You will only have to look at the lists of names and types of bedding dahlias provided at the end of this chapter to realize the great variety of schemes that could be adopted.

One type of bedding design involves using taller dahlias as well. 'Bishop of Llandaff', for instance, which may grow 3ft high, and which has glorious scarlet flowers and deep bronze-purple leaves, could be used as a centrepiece of any bed. In fact I have seen it used with great success at Hampton Court. One or more of the dwarfer varieties would then be planted around, acting as foils to the main centre attraction. So one could choose, from the lists in Chapter 12, certain varieties to use in the centre of a bedding scheme, and then concentrate on the varieties listed at the end of this chapter for the main feature of the bedding.

The Organization of Bedding Out

The whole point of using dahlias is to get a glorious show of flowers during the whole of the summer, say from June to October. When they are planted out from their pots at the end of May, or early in June, they may easily have a flower on them. It is inadvisable to leave them in the ground after the middle of October, even if the frost has not cut them down, because by that time one will need to plant out a winter or spring bedding scheme. Most people want to have a good display, the following spring, of wallflowers, forget-me-nots, or polyanthus, plus, perhaps, a mass effect of early tulips, and to do this it is necessary to get the beds planted sufficiently early in the autumn.

Some readers may wonder what 'bedding out' really means. It can be defined as a system of planting out groups of plants of a similar colour which will bloom at a certain time, or over a definite period. Bedding out creates formality, and so it is used for borders near the house, or for formal gardens that are perhaps purposely sunk, or perhaps arranged on the level and surrounded by grass or stone paving.

In the gardens of small modern villas the more formal beds at the front of the house are usually bedded out, as are the long narrow beds lining the path to the front door. Bedding, therefore, is the planting out of free-flowering plants that will give a glorious colourful display: dahlias may be used for the summer, and wallflowers or forget-me-nots for the spring.

When the beds are surrounded by grass the greatest care must be taken to see that the edges are trimmed regularly throughout the spring and summer. Otherwise they will look very untidy. On light sandy soils the edges of the beds may be allowed to become a little rough during the winter, and then in the spring be cut back with the sharp edge of a semi-circular turfing iron. This will consolidate the edges. Some people purposely have a tiled edging to a bed, so that they do not have to worry about the constant cutting back and trimming of the grass.

It is always necessary to start planning your bedding a year or so in advance. Only in this way can you tell exactly the number of plants you will need to raise, or to order from the local nurseryman, to carry out your scheme. I always raise more plants than I need, so that (a) I can fill up any gaps that appear as the result of some accident or disease, and (b) I can be reasonably discriminating when it comes to planting out, and choose plants of similar height and growth.

Preparation of the Bed

One needs to take a fair amount of trouble with the preparation of the beds in which these bedding dahlias are going to be planted. The great danger is that the ground never gets a chance of being properly forked or manured. One kind of plant is taken out late in the spring to accommodate the summer bedding and then suddenly in October it is necessary to whip out the summer bedding to make room for the spring-flowering plants.

As far as dahlias are concerned it is inadvisable to fork in quantities of farmyard manure or dung before planting, but on the other hand failures may occur if the soil is lacking in organic matter. It is therefore a good thing to fork damp sedge peat into the beds if the soil is dry. Do this in the spring, applying the sedge peat at the rate of a bucketful to the square yard. Fish manure may be raked in at the same time, at 4 oz to the square yard. If the soil is wet at the time the peat should not be damped beforehand.

If the ground appears to be dry (and with formal beds it so often is), it may be advisable to water the beds thoroughly before carrying out any forking or manuring. Firm soil always takes water more quickly than land that is puffy and loose. A good flooding may make all the difference to the plants, even though there may be a droughty period later on. Use, if possible, a square area rainer on a hose attached to the tap and give the land artificial rain for, say, a couple of hours.

Preparation of the Plants

The plants that you are going to put out in the beds should be watered the day before, whether they are growing in pots or in boxes.

It is always better to plant out dahlias with as good a ball of soil attached to the roots as possible. If, therefore, the plants are in boxes, prepare them a couple of days before planting. Take a sharp knife and use this to cut the soil in between the plants, firstly down the whole length of the box and secondly from side to side. This should leave each plant growing in a square of soil. Give the boxes a good watering, and then, when the time comes a day or two later to get the plants out of the boxes, the square of soil should come out neatly with the roots of the plant.

Planting

Start planting the outside rows of the bed and then the corners, whether the plants come out of a box, as has been suggested, or out of 3-in. pots. Using a trowel, make a good hole that will easily take the ball of soil, pop the roots in and firm them well with the handle of the trowel. Do not actually press against the stem of the dahlia. Instead, press all round the outside of the ball of soil so that it is really well bedded in.

As has already been said, it is advisable to plant rather thickly in order to ensure a massed effect later, and so in the normal way bedding dahlias may be set out 18 in. square. Where large beds are to be planted, it is convenient to use a short plank to step on or kneel on. This prevents leaving deep heel marks or, of course, knee marks. By moving the plank backwards, when working from one side of the bed to the other, it is possible to plant up and then tidy up the beds as you go.

Once the dahlias are all firmly planted in position, set up an overhead sprinkler in the centre of the bed. Attach the sprinkler to a rubber or plastic hose and then turn on the tap. This will give the soil a thorough soaking. Generally speaking, it is advisable to leave the overhead sprinkler in position for half an hour, but in a dry year, and with very sandy soil, it may be necessary to soak for an hour, and then follow this with a mulching of sedge peat.

Maintenance

Once the bedding dahlias are in position there is little more to be done other than an occasional hoeing in the early stages, to keep down the weeds. Eventually the spread of the foliage makes this quite unnecessary. Keep a sharp lookout for pests and diseases, and take the necessary precautions or methods of control as recommended in Chapter 15. As a matter of routine, pick off all the heads immediately they have finished flowering, to prevent seed pods from forming. This regular removal of old flowers helps the plants to go on blooming regularly, and prevents the bed from looking unsightly.

There will be no need to feed bedding dahlias during the summer, they can be allowed to grow quite naturally. It is in the spring, when the ground is prepared, that all the necessary plant foods should be incorporated in the soil. Bearing in mind the fact that the whole purpose of bedding out is to get a mass of colour, rather than green leaf, over as long a period as possible, the gardener will concentrate on feeding the ground with plenty of phosphates and potash, and allow only a minimum of nitrogen.

Varieties

There are very many Dwarf Dahlias to use for bedding. I have given their names in alphabetical order, but some are Singles, some might be described as Mignons, some as Doubles, and others as Half-Doubles. They come from various groups. 'Midget', for instance, is really a Small Cactus, but as it only grows 1 ft high, I have included it under the heading of 'bedding varieties'. The same applies also to 'Plentiful', which is really a Small Decorative, but which again only grows 1 ft high.

Balgay	– pink and yellow blends
Border Prince	– lilac, very prolific
Border Princess	– orange, most popular for all schemes
Border Triumph	– bright flame orange
Bridesmaid	– white, anenome
Brielle	– yellow, semi-cactus
Brio	– flame coloured, anenome
Broad Oak Bedder	– pink, with fimbriated petals
Butterball	– yellow, one of the best
Christine Caldwell	– orange blends, decorative
Clova	– deep purple, decorative
Coltness Gem	– seed-sown singles, very colourful
Cordial	– flame coloured, cactus
Corona	– good red, decorative
Croll's Bedder	– shades of red and purple

Dalhousie Peach	– larger bloom, pink and yellow
Downham	– a bedder to beat them all, yellow
Elburg	– Dutch, orange, decorative
Ella Britten	– orange and red blends in this beauty
Exotic Dwarf	– a 'Topmix' variety, the smallest dahlias of all, pink
Fabel	– light pink and white
Facet	– bronze, single-flowered
Fascination	– very popular, light mauve, paeony-flowered
Frank Soeton	– pure cactus form, white, excellent variety
Gaiety	– bronze and pink, decorative
Golden Pride	– orange and yellow blends
Granato	– flame, anenome
Honey	– pink and yellow, a real stunner
Inflammation	– single bedder, bright red
Janet Miner	– pink and yellow, semi-cactus
Jean Thompson	– red and dark pink, decorative
Jessie Ross	– deepest pink, decorative
Kendal Gem	– an orange beauty from the Lake District
Lawside	– lilac, decorative
Little Drummer Boy	– red 'Topmix', very prolific
Maggies Favourite	– red blends, anenome
Mariette	– red and yellow, anenome
Maureen Creighton	– dark red, decorative
Michigan	– very short bush, orange and red bi-colour
Nellie Geerlings	– a famous bedder, red, single
New Fun	– orange, decorative
Orange Flora	– orange with some yellow, paeony-flowered
Park Delight	– white, semi-cactus
Park Jewel	– dark pink, cactus
Park Princess	– truly a princess – the finest bedder of all time, pink
Park Wonder	– another in the Park range, yellow
Piper's Pink	– this Norfolk-raised beauty is a winner, pink, cactus
Princess Marie Jose	– lavender, single, a favourite at Harrogate Parks

Red Dwarf	– attractive red single, habit as name
Red Imp	– colour as name, decorative
Rocquencourt	– flame with bronze foliage, decorative,
Rothesay Castle	– the Rothesays are Scottish-raised, this one pink and white
Rothesay Herald	– red and white
Rothesay Yellow	– one of the best bedding yellows
Siemen Doorenbos	– Dutch, lilac and white, anemone
Sweet Autumn	– orange blends, decorative
Wee Jean	– a lovely little white bedder
Windermere	– a grand red for your border
Yellow Cheer	– colour as name, a good single
Yellow Hammer	– a famous bedder, single and prolific.

10 Showing Dahlias

Readers who become very enthusiastic about dahlia growing may find themselves with a great desire to enter some of their flowers in a local horticultural show. From a local show they may graduate perhaps to a county show, until at last one day they find themselves putting up a wonderful exhibit at the National Dahlia Society's own show in the hall of the Royal Horticultural Society in London. It is surprising what can be done by gardeners who are really interested and keen, and I have known people with only two or three years' experience gain premier awards. In earlier days dahlias were usually shown cut, with the blooms lying flat on special trays provided for the purpose. The reason for this was that so many of the large dahlia flowers growing in the border could not hold up their heads, and so had a rather 'hang-dog' look about them. With the flowering heads cut off, and little stems inserted into special cups of water which were fitted to holes in trays, the flowers could be shown to advantage. At most shows today, however, dahlias are exhibited as cut blooms with long stems.

There are, of course, certain varieties which are particularly useful for exhibition purposes, and if you are intending to go in for showing you should certainly spend much of your spare time the previous year in going round all the horticultural shows within call, so that you can note down the names of varieties and discover for yourself what has satisfied and pleased the judges.

You will not be allowed in the tent or hall while the judging is going on, but it is usually possible, at local and county shows, to walk in before judging time and to see the dahlia experts at work. Everybody will be far too busy to take any notice of you, but you can make notes on how the staging is done, the kinds of vase that are used, the amount of water that is put in, the cutting off of an inch, say, from the base of the stems, the burning of the new stem base with a match, and all the many tricks of the trade. If you join a local horticultural society, you will be sent a schedule of the various show classes in plenty of time, so you will know when to go and what to look for.

As far as the growing of the dahlias is concerned, there is very little necessity to alter the general culture, except, perhaps, in the case of Pompon varieties. Care must be taken with these so that the blooms are as near perfectly spherical as possible. The centres must never be sunken, and they should look perfect. One can seldom get such blooms on land that has been richly manured, especially when the plants have been correctly thinned to reduce the number of blooms per plant to around eight, and when correct disbudding has been done. Pompons for show, in fact, should be grown rather hard. They must never be given too much water, and they should not be fed.

Protecting Show Blooms

Fortunately, the colours of Pompons seldom fade, but as those of the larger types of flowers often do, special methods of shading must be adopted. Shades will protect the flowers not only from bright sunshine, but also from heavy rain or dew; drops of moisture may easily cause blemishes. A whole bed of dahlias being grown for show can be shaded and protected by a sheet of butter muslim, held in position over the bed by some kind of wooden frame. Some gardeners use polythene for this purpose, but this has the disadvantage of not letting any moisture through at all, and also, after a heavy rainfall, the weight of water may easily split or displace the temporary polythene cover.

In this country many people successfully protect their show blooms with conical-shaped 'hats' made of thick brown paper and wire. The size of the 'hats' will vary in accordance with the size of the bloom. If, for instance, a dahlia is going to be 11 or 12 in. across – as some of the largest specimens can be – then the base of the hat or cone should be about 18 in. across. What are really needed are specially shaped lampshades which will last and stand the weather. In Rhodesia and South Africa, where baskets are made very cheaply, it is possible to protect individual blooms with inverted baskets of a special shape. These give ideal protection from the sun and rain as well as the necessary amount of ventilation.

One needn't be fussy about making special hats. I once visited one of my client's gardens and found all the dahlias being protected with twenty or thirty old umbrellas. These are, of course, ideal for the purpose, but they present quite a problem when there are gales about. People who don't mind what their gardens look like as long as they have perfect dahlia blooms will be able to consider using large cardboard boxes, light 3-ply trays, and in fact anything that will provide shade and protection and may be fixed over the blooms when they start to unfold.

It is not only from the sun, the wind and the rain that the flowers must be protected. Earwigs and maybe caterpillars too will undoubtedly be present. Many of the pests that attack dahlia blooms are nocturnal, and one can trap them in 3-in. pots filled with straw or woodwool and placed upside down on the bamboos or sticks used for supporting the dahlias. Remove each pot every morning, put two fingers over the loose contents, and then tap the pot into a little tin of paraffin. The insect creatures will be dislodged and killed in the paraffin. It helps also if derris is dusted around the base of the plants, to discourage pests from visiting the plants in the first place.

With longer-stemmed varieties, and especially those that have quite heavy flower heads, it is worth taking the trouble to tie a thin bamboo to each stem, to support and reinforce it. This will prevent breakages in high winds. These bamboos, of course, will be removed when the stems are put into the vases for exhibition.

Filling in the Forms

Before you send in your exhibit it will be necessary to obtain an entrance form from the Secretary and fill it in correctly. Make up your mind in which classes you would like to compete. It does not matter if you make an entry for an extra class or two which, when the time comes, you cannot enter because of lack of suitable flowers. Do not, however, let the side down more than you need because the Secretary will have kept the space for your exhibit, and if you do not compete in a particular class it makes the exhibits on the tabling look rather thin.

When sending the entry form to the Secretary, be sure to enclose a cheque or postal order covering the entry fees. Fill in your name and address carefully, preferably in capital letters, since there is nothing more annoying to any secretary than to receive forms with no name on them or with names and addresses that cannot be read.

See that you read the schedule very carefully indeed, for the judges will stick by this. It's a very bad mistake to misread it and then argue with the Secretary when the day comes. Make a note of the classes that you have pledged yourself to compete in, and then make sure that you have the necessary plants and varieties so that there will be no difficulty on the day of the show. If, for example, the show schedule is very definite and insists on Collarette single dahlias, then you must be sure that you have got Collarette singles.

Don't be afraid to take the form to the Secretary and fill it up in his presence. He will be able to advise and help you, and will probably let you have the schedule of last year's show. You cannot have a show without exhibitors, and a Secretary who is worth his salt is always anxious to encourage new people. He will be glad to help you months before the show, but he will be much too busy to do anything for you on the day or even, perhaps, during the week before.

Early Planning

Having decided on which classes you are going to enter, it would be well worth while discussing the varieties you are going to grow with other exhibitors and with your favourite nurseryman. There are always varieties that seem to do better at shows than others, and a good nurseryman will know best. It's essential, of course, to deal with a man on whose judgement you can rely, and who will send you plants in good condition and at the right time.

Decide early on how many plants will be required; it's really surprising how many plants are needed even to put up a vase of six flowers. The dahlia is very floriferous and one plant may carry twenty blooms or more, depending on the variety, and yet very often, when you're trying to cut six good flowers, all of the same size, shape and colour shade, you may find great difficulty in obtaining what you need on one plant. It is most important to see that each bloom is just as good as another. It is no good having five perfect flowers and one that is twisted or speckled. Each flower must be the exact replica of the next one, like peas in a pod. It is essential, therefore, to have four or five plants of every variety that you hope to include on the show bench.

Beginners at showing will be well advised, in the first year, to aim for one class only, and grow about a dozen pots of the right variety for this class. This will enable them to take to the show a large number of spares in case of accidents. Once a start has been made, one can go in for three or four classes the next year, and probably reduce the number of plants required for each one.

The Judging

The judges' decision, of course, is final. As one who has judged at many shows up and down the country, I can assure you that judges do their best and that they are bound by rules drawn up by the Royal Horticultural Society in conjunction with the National Dahlia Society. They award points for (a) quality, (b) freshness, (c) size, and (d) arrangement, so you will realize that it is not necessarily size that carries the awards every time. What matters most is the quality of the blooms, and whether they are really perfect and fresh. The flowers should be at the right angle on a good stem, and arranged so that they can be seen easily. (The judges pay attention to the back florets because sometimes these are plucked when they have started to fade.) There is also a size limit to take account of. This is set by the National Dahlia Society's classification and must be adhered to scrupulously.

Incidentally, the footstalk is an important part to consider when showing dahlias for competitions. This is the part between the bloom and the first true leaf. By national standards it should be over 10 in. long.

Don't worry if you don't win a prize the first year because nobody will be worrying about you. People always look for the names on the prize-winners' card, and so if you haven't won your name won't be noticed and you need never feel ashamed. People are often discouraged when their plants seem to have had an 'off-week' just about the time of the show. They look marvellous the week before and wonderful the week after, but at the very time you need the best blooms the plants seem to be doing their worst! However clever you are, this can happen, so don't be dismayed. Don't be a grumbler, be a sport, and if you fail to win the first time, try, try, try again!

Disqualifications

Exhibits will be disqualified for any of the following reasons:

1. Blooms of Large-flowered Dahlias exceeding 260 mm (10¼ in.).
   Blooms of Medium-flowered Dahlias exceeding 220 mm (8¾ in.).
   Blooms of Small-flowered Dahlias exceeding 170 mm (6¾ in.).
   Blooms of Miniature-flowered Dahlias exceeding 115 mm (4½ in.).
   Blooms of Pompon Dahlias exceeding 50 mm (2 in.).

2. Blooms artificially supported above the top of the vase.

3. Incorrect number of blooms in an exhibit.

4. Classified blooms exhibited in wrong class.

5. If a vase in a multi-vase exhibit should be not as scheduled, then the whole exhibit must be disqualified. Once an exhibit has been disqualified, it cannot be considered for any other award, either in whole or in part.

To measure the sizes of the dahlias on show, the judges should use rings approved by the National Dahlia Society. The florets of blooms exhibited must pass cleanly through the inner perimeter of the ring without distortion of the bloom.

Practising Beforehand

It is very necessary to practise arranging the dahlias in vases a week or two before the show. Practise with flowers of a similar size to those you are going to display, and with stems of a similar thickness. It's quite hard to arrange dahlias in a vase with the flowers all facing one way. You could use thick dahlia stems, cut into lengths, to wedge the stems of the show blooms, but there are other materials to use which will be mentioned later.

If you are showing six small Pompons, these should be arranged in the form of a pyramid, with three blooms in the bottom row, two blooms above this, and the last bloom in the centre of the two, just above them. To carry out this arrangement it may be necessary to adjust the lengths of the stems. The dahlias themselves must not touch one another, and above the water level of the vase the leaves should be left on the stem.

Staging exhibition dahlias can be tricky. Note how these vases have been symmetrically arranged

Read the schedule carefully before you practise because sometimes you will find the words 'to be arranged for effect'. In this case it would be unwise to try the pyramid idea because a pleasing, more natural arrangement is required. Once again, at the risk of boring the reader, may I advise him or her to go to a few dahlia shows and see how arrangement for effect is done. The best way to learn this type of work is to see it and not merely to read about it in a book. Most dahlia shows, by the way, are held in August or September.

Exhibiting according to Schedule

One of the saddest things I have had to do when judging is to disqualify an entry which otherwise would have easily won the first prize. Do make certain that the dahlias you are putting into a particular class conform absolutely to the instructions given clearly on the schedule. You must have the right number of blooms, they must be of the right type, and the vase must be placed in the right spot. It is very easy to make a mistake if you are entering in two or more classes. Exhibit A can easily be placed in Class B by mistake, in the excitement of the moment.

Cutting and Preparing the Blooms

It is always sensible to pick a much greater number of dahlia blooms than will actually be needed for the exhibit, then if there are any disasters with the flowers between the garden and the show bench, there will be some spares to fill in. Cut the dahlias with as long a stem as possible and always do this when the stems are surfeited with moisture. In a dry year, therefore, it may be necessary to give the dahlia bed a really good soaking with water two or three days beforehand.

Never cut in the middle of the day when the sun is up. I prefer to do the work in the evening, but some people prefer to cut very early in the morning, and there are some experts who cut at night-time, when it is quite dark; to do this they have to mark the flowers they are going to remove.

Be sure that the blade of the knife is really sharp, and make a clean cut across the stem. (With the largest varieties the stem should be about 2 ft long.) Remove the lower leaves immediately with the knife, taking care not to cut into the stem, and put the flowers into water as soon as possible. The best method is to carry out to the dahlia bed a deep bucket half-filled with water. In this way there is no danger of an air-lock forming in the stems. Dahlias that are cut and then taken into the kitchen or shed after a delay of half an hour or so, may easily suffer as a result. Moisture continues to rise up the stem, once the stem has been cut, and air follows. When the stem is plunged into water again an air-lock is produced near the base of the stem. If this should happen, the solution is to cut off an inch of the stem below water, making the cut slanting instead of horizontal.

To eliminate air-locks when plunging blooms, or when staging at shows, and to ensure maximum uptake of water, carefully insert the tip of a knife-blade just below each joint of the stem that is *under water,* taking care not to penetrate so far as to weaken the stem. Give a slight twist, and you will observe numerous air bubbles rising. Ensure that all air is excluded. A nail file is an even better tool, as it does not cut the stem when twisted.

If the show is on Saturday, cut the blooms on Friday evening, Friday night, or very early on Saturday morning. If you have difficulty with some varieties which seem to refuse to take up water when cut, you can dip the ends of the stems in boiling water for about twelve seconds, or about seven seconds if the stems are narrow. After this dipping the dahlias should be stood in a deep bucket or vase of water, and they will then continue to take in the moisture they need.

Remember that blooms continue to mature and expand after cutting, so do not cut blooms that have reached maximum expansion unless you can get them to the show within half a day, otherwise the back petals will begin to fade.

From Home to Show

People who are exhibiting a dozen blooms or so should have no difficulty in transporting them in water. This is ideal because then air-locks cannot occur during the journey. Perhaps there is space in the back of a motor car for vases to be arranged in such a way that the blooms travel perfectly, without damage. I have known people in the country take their dahlias to the local show in a pram, or in a special little hard-cart made for the purpose.

It's only when you become quite an expert at showing, and decide that you will compete in the national shows, that you have to consider using special cases in which the blooms lie flat, with rubber or plastic balloons full of water tied over the ends of the stems, to keep the flowers fresh during the move. Once again, one can learn much by going early to a big show in order to see how the other exhibitors pack their dahlias, and what schemes they adopt to make certain that the flowers arrive in perfect condition. Some people pack their dahlias with a certain amount of cotton wool to prevent bruising, and this is particularly necessary with Pompon varieties.

Perhaps the best way to transport large blooms is to use a milkman's bottle crate. A large one will accommodate five blooms, clear of each other, with one in each corner and one in the centre. Each bloom will be in water in a milk bottle, with a cane tied to the stem and to the crate and with cotton wool padding at the ties.

To eliminate the effects of shaking while travelling is most important. One easy method is to use large distemper drums and carefully pack these to capacity. There is some danger, however, of florets getting misplaced or otherwise damaged.

On the Day

The dahlias have been successfully transported from your garden. You arrive at the show with great excitement, and when you have carefully parked your exhibits you should go straight away to the Secretary's table or tent in order to get your entry cards. Incidentally, it is a good idea to take an assistant with you on such occasions. The assistant should stand by the exhibits to make certain that they are not damaged while you are obtaining the cards, and discovering exactly where your exhibit or exhibits should be placed.

Be alert, and don't allow another exhibitor to 'winkle' you out of the spot that the committee has allotted to you. Old hands are very cunning at this. They like to have their exhibit at the front of the bench, and if they can push yours to the back they will do so. It's therefore well worth your while to hang about after you have put up your exhibit until the call of 'everybody out', which is when the judges will begin their work.

Take care not to arrange the flowers on the bench where they are going to be displayed. Nice white paper will probably have been placed on the bench and if you do the stem cutting, defoliating and arranging there, you are sure to make an untidy mess! Find a spot in the corner of the room or tent, arrange the vase, and then when it's correct, and nice and clean, put it into position. Always keep your spare blooms to hand until the judging actually starts, in case of a last-minute mishap.

It may be necessary to take to the show some kind of material to put in the bottom of the vases, so that the stems of the blooms will 'stay put' when placed in position. One could use lengths of thick dahlia stalk, about 4 in. long, or lengths of green sedge such as one finds in damp ground. Some experts prepare wooden wedges, and push these down into the vases as the stems are placed into position, to keep them firm. Other experts use damp moss very successfully. It is advisable to get the arranging and wedging done quickly before the water is put in.

A wise exhibitor will take with him to the show a large watering can with a long spout, so that he always has water available for filling his vases *in situ*. Taps are often scarce at shows, and exhibitors who are waiting to fill individual vases, because they have not brought a large can, may easily find themselves in a long queue.

It was mentioned earlier on that when a number of similar blooms are required, these are best arranged in tiers. On the other hand, if the schedule asks for three large blooms, then these are usually arranged in a fan shape, say at an angle of forty-five degrees. Sometimes only one giant bloom is called for, and this should be sited right in the centre of a strong, firmly-based vase.

Incidentally, green vases are usually preferred by judges, and special types with wide mouths, narrower waists and wide bases can be obtained from horticultural sundriesmen. They are made especially for this purpose. Even a vase of this type may topple over if the staging provided by the show committee is not absolutely level. So if you find that this is the case, speak to a steward immediately or make a complaint to the Secretary.

Labelling

It is helpful to provide a small label, probably no more than $1\frac{1}{2}$ in. by 1 in., on which the name of the variety can be very carefully printed. Attach this to a small length of wire and, if possible, hook the wire over the lip of the vase; it will remain in position even if the judge lifts your exhibit to examine it from the underside. Clearly named, the vases are of great interest to those who will be visiting the show once the judging is over. Of course, if there is a rule in the schedule about not naming, you must obey the instructions.

After the Judging

The moment the judging is over and the public are again admitted, you will naturally be anxious to discover whether or not you have won a prize. If you have not been lucky, please don't be disappointed, but do everything you can to learn from your failure. Look at the prize-winning exhibits and see whether you can discover for yourself why you have been beaten. If you cannot do so, try and get one of the stewards to come and explain the points of perfection to you. At smaller shows the judges are often there for some time and if you go politely to one of them, and he sees that you are not moaning or groaning but really wanting to learn, then he will often be kind enough to return to the bench and explain to you clearly why a particular vase of dahlias was better than another.

He may start by enthusing on the formation of the blooms, their symmetrical outline, and perfect centres. He may point out the even or uneven arrangement of the florets, or that there are far too few florets to make the bloom look perfect. He may also mention colour. Dahlia flowers can vary enormously in this respect: for instance, reds that have been grown in bright sun may not be as brilliant as blooms of the same variety grown with a certain amount of protection.

If the schedule says that you may show twelve distinct varieties, then you may have lost a point or two by not realizing the advantage of including a number of different colours.

He will probably point out the value of a nice strong stem, and will show you how the prize-winning blooms are poised on these stems at the right angle. He will undoubtedly mention freshness, and maybe point to a back floret on one of your dahlias which has wilted, unknown to you. Something may be said about the healthy foliage on the stems. He may also draw your attention to an excellent little booklet issued by the National Dahlia Society, called *The Classified List of Dahlias and Guide for Judges.* This can be obtained, price 40p, from Mr Philip Damp, 26 Burns Road, Lillington, Leamington Spa.

11 Cactus and Semi-cactus Dahlias

It is said that the original Cactus Dahlia came from Mexico in 1872. It arrived on the Continent and proved to be a highly developed, cultivated variety, and not at all like the wild dahlias that had come from Mexico in previous years. It was named *Dahli juarezii*, after the President of Mexico whose name was Signor Juarez. Because it has a resemblance, so it was thought in those days, to the blooms of the cactus, somebody suggested that it should be known as a 'Cactus Dahlia'. But whether this name was given in Mexico or France, no-one seems to know.

The Cactus Dahlia was first introduced into England in the 1880s by Henry Cannell, a very go-ahead business man who obtained some plants from a private gardener in London and propagated them extensively. I understand that these dahlias were the first exhibited in 1880.

This *juarezii* was a true double, the petals being long, narrow and straight, but not strikingly revolute as they are today. The stem was strong and good. After a year or so a purple spot arose which proved to be popular, this being named 'Beauty of Arundel' after the Duke of Norfolk's home. Soon it was discovered that seeds could be obtained from *juarezii* and then of course many different colours and varieties were produced.

At the Crystal Palace, between 1890 and 1900, you could have attended a dahlia show once a year. In those days only four types were available: Single, Pompon, Show and Cactus Dahlias. The flowers were exhibited in bunches of three, six or ten on wire frames, and veterans to whom I have spoken about these shows say that the exhibits were truly wonderful.

It was at this time that Cactus Dahlias became very fashionable indeed and many leading raisers aimed at producing new varieties with narrow revolute petals. Alas, the Cactus eventually fell into disrepute, apparently because they were supposed to have weak stems.

So growers and raisers went on breeding Cactus Dahlias, with the result that many new types arose. It is said, though I never saw one, that there was a stout, erect, free-flowering type of Cactus Dahlia produced at one time. One raiser, the late Harry Stredwick of Silverhill Park, used the Cactus Dahlia as the male parent and the Double Show as the female, and produced Giant Dahlias which created quite a stir at the time. These dahlias were often 9 ft high, the blooms could be $14\frac{1}{2}$ in. across and the large leaves, it was said, were 2 ft 3 in. long. They certainly could breed them in those days!

The word 'revolute' should be explained. It means 'rolled backwards' or, as some people put it 'quilled'. The petals of these dahlias are always pointed and sometimes incurved. Sometimes the petals are so tightly rolled that they have been likened to the spindly legs of spiders, so that at least one variety has been given the name 'Giant Spider'.

As you examine the various Cactus Dahlias you will find that the flowers vary and so do the individual petals. In most cases the quilling is complete, but sometimes the petals seem to be only slightly rolled back. It was for this reason that, in the days of the veteran Harry Stredwick, Cactus Dahlias were divided into (a) Fully Double Semi-Cactus (b) Single Cactus (c) Small Semi-Double Cactus and (d) Large True Cactus. It was obviously difficult for any expert to decide on border-line varieties. There were, in fact, plants that would one year produce blooms that appeared to be definitely Cactus and then the following season, perhaps because of the weather, or the soil or the manure, blooms that seemed to be in the Decorative Class.

Not every country, of course, abides by the classifications laid down by our National Dahlia Society, as I have discovered on my advisory trips abroad in Europe, Canada and the United States. The various Cactus Dahlias can be divided into what are called 'straight-cactus' and 'incurved-cactus' types.

It is interesting also to note that the forking at the tip of the petals of some types of Cactus Dahlias is looked upon in Australia and New Zealand as a defect, but in Canada, on the other hand, in the United States, and in Europe, there are many different forked varieties and they are becoming increasingly popular. With these laciniated Cactus Dahlias, as the Americans call them, the split in the petals can be from $\frac{1}{4}$ in. to $1\frac{1}{2}$ in. long. The illustration on page 000 will show you how feathery these dahlias look.

The variety called 'Progenitor', which the National Dahlia Society mention in their 1904 Yearbook as being furcated (or forked), was undoubtedly one of the first of these laciniated varieties. Whether in the long run there will be a special group or classification allowed for these varieties, I do not know.

If the true Cactus varieties have a fault, it is that there may be too few individual florets, with the result that the flower is a bit skimped. Sometimes, unfortunately, the individual florets or petals are not evenly distributed around the centre of the flower, and then show judges will describe them as 'gappy'. The perfect Cactus Dahlia should have its florets or petals evenly distributed right around the centre of the blooms, radiating perfectly like the rays of the sun in all directions. There should be a fair depth of bloom, as well as width, and, if you are intending to show them, the florets should be even, rather than a mixture of flattened and revolute.

If you turn back to Chapter 2, you will see that Cactus Dahlias are currently included in Group IX. It is stated officially that Cactus Dahlias have fully double flowers, showing no central disc. The majority of ray florets are usually pointed, narrower than those of Decorative Dahlias, revolute for a part of their length, and either straight or incurving.

A list of the various Cactus Dahlias with descriptions is given below, but since new varieties are introduced almost every year it will soon be slightly out-of-date. Not all the varieties listed will be obtainable from one nurseryman, but I would always be willing to give the names and addresses of growers in various parts of the country, and if you join the National Dahlia Society you will find that nurserymen advertise in the official booklets and the yearly magazine.

Varieties

These lists of Cactus Dahlias are in accordance with the classifications of the National Dahlia Society. It has been impossible to mention every variety, but the majority of those that are beautiful as well as reliable have been included.

GIANT-FLOWERED CACTUS (over 10 in. in diameter)

Apex	– orange and bronze, a spiky beauty
Danny	– mid-pink from the USA
Grand Geste	– needle-sharp florets on this giant golden Cactus
Polar Sight	– white from Holland, one of the top varieties

GIANT-FLOWERED SEMI-CACTUS (over 10 in. in diameter)

Arab Queen	– pink and yellow, really massive

Bizet – a new arrival from Holland, pink and apricot, massive
Croeso – another giant pink from Wales
Dinah Shore – this lovely lavender is from the USA
Eightieth Birthday – brilliant red, another good newcomer
Frontispiece – exhibition white with fimbriated petals
Genius – light purple, well-formed
Goody Goody – blooms a foot across, pale yellow
Persian Monarch – dark pink, a tall-growing winner
Pop Stretton – from 'down under', this pink and yellow is very popular
Respectable – the best giant semi of them all, easy to grow, orange
Sei Ki – a tremendous red from Japan, blooms 14 in. wide
Surprise – blooms wide and deep in this top variety from the USA
Yukikemuri – pure white from Japan

LARGE-FLOWERED SEMI-CACTUS (8–10 in. in diameter)

Alden Alpine – Australian white
Buoyance – apricot, a newcomer that is already popular, Dutch
Eldorado – orange tipped white bicolour
Holland Herald – flame, a top show winner
Hamari Katrina – palest yellow from Britain's top raiser, Mr Ensum
Hamari Princess – pastel yellow, tipped mauve, a lovely dahlia
Luxury – bright flame-red on strong stems
Nantenan – in my view the best dahlia since the War, bright yellow
Olympic Torch – light orange and powerful stems, all-purpose
Paul Critchley – pink, raised in the north of England
Quel Diable – flame blooms on strong bush
Reginald Keene – blends, light orange buff and some yellow, a top dahlia

MEDIUM-FLOWERED CACTUS AND SEMI-CACTUS (6–8 in. in diameter)

Amelisweerd (SC) – buff, from Holland, a popular dahlia
Curtain Raiser (C) – light bronze, a superb variety

'Holland Festival'

Eastwood Delight (SC)	– pink and yellow blends, from Essex
Elmbridge (SC)	– top winner, a yellow newcomer of merit
Hamari Bride (SC)	– the best white medium of all
Hamari Sunset (SC)	– from Mr Ensum, colour as name, a beauty
Othello (SC)	– the darkest red of all, almost black
Radiance (C)	– a lovely shade of pink for the garden
Spiky Symbol	– a form sport of the famous Symbol, buff
Symbol (SC)	– perhaps the best medium ever raised

'Purple Globe'

12 Decorative Dahlias

If it were ever possible to write the full history of the dahlia, and to give a full account of what happened in the very early days, I think it would be discovered that the Decorative Dahlia, as we know it today, is very similar to the Double-flowered Dahlia that grew in Mexico hundreds of years ago. Double-flowered varieties were introduced into Europe in the early part of the nineteenth century and it is probably true that experts in those days were able to breed further varieties. Decorative Dahlias are now very popular, but sixty years ago they were the most popular type of dahlia grown, according to the old gardeners I used to know.

Decorative Dahlias developed naturally from paeony-flowered varieties that had partly flat petals, but then the Ball Dahlia evolved from much the same parentage. Other blood must have been introduced, including small varieties of Ball Dahlias and large varieties of Paeony-flowered Dahlias.

Decorative Dahlias, of course, have fully double flowers, showing no disc at all. The ray florets are usually broad, more or less flat or slightly twisted, and are generally bluntly pointed. They are scarcely revolute at all. As Chapter 2 shows, there are various classes of Decorative Dahlias, Giant-flowered, Large-flowered, Medium-flowered, Small-flowered and Miniature-flowered. All these various types can be had in many different colours, and in the Small-flowered group there are literally dozens of varieties that are grown successfully for cut flowers.

One can find dahlias listed in the official dahlia handbook under the heading Decoratives, which in fact appear to be very nearly Cactus types. Many differently shaped flowers, some of them almost globular or round, and others flatter and shallower, come within this classification. The main difference between the Decorative and the Cactus types is the fact that Cactus types have revolute petals or florets, which means that they are shaped like the quills of a porcupine. Decoratives, on the other hand, have flatter petals.

In the classification set out in Chapter 2 dimensions are given for the various types. Medium-flowered Decorative Dahlias, for instance, normally have flowers between 6 in. and 8 in. in diameter. And yet differences do occur when dahlias are specially disbuded, or when they are grown and fed in a particular manner.

Some Decoratives, and particularly some in the Miniature-flowered group, can be used for bedding. I have heard a housewife say that if she can persuade her husband to bed out the front garden with Dwarf Miniature-flowered Jescots, not only can she be sure of having a wonderful show up to the end of September, but also she will have plenty of cut flowerers for the house. Solid, well-grown blooms of Decoratives will last wonderfully well in water, especially if they have been stood with water up to their necks for two or three hours, to strengthen the stems before arranging.

It would be very difficult to make an arbitrary choice among all the Decorative varieties, for inclusion in this book. So all I have done is to list, under the various headings, a large number of Decorative Dahlias that are known to be successful in many different parts of this country, as well as in Canada, Southern Africa, New Zealand, Gibraltar, etc.

Varieties

The classifications given below are those of the National Dahlia Society. Naturally I have not been able to include every single variety, but I have chosen ones that are both beautiful and easy to grow.

GIANT-FLOWERED DECORATIVES (over 10 in. in diameter)

Air Marshal	– pink, easily grown, from Holland
Almand's Climax	– lavender and white, a New Zealand beauty
Alvas Supreme	– pale yellow, finishes like a ball, from New Zealand
Annette	– a veteran yellow, still good
Atlantic	– bright red on good stems
Barbara Shann	– flame, an informal petalled beauty
Black Monarch	– from the USA, a dark red monster bloom
Bonafide	– from Holland, one of the best yellows

Bramley's Sunset	– raised recently, sunset colours, and very good
Bronze Liberator	– bronze sport of the famous Australian 'Liberator'
Cherokee Beauty	– pink, a deeply-formed giant from the USA
Corton Trudy	– palest yellow, new and promising
Countryman	– Dutch-raised, bronze, really big
Crossfield Masterpiece	– blends of pink and yellow
Croydon Masterpiece	– Australian, one of the finest giants ever
Croydon Superior	– a fairly recent arrival, pink and yellow
Elmbrook Chieftain	– red and yellow, a recent British introduction
Emory Paul	– purple and massive, from the USA
Encinitas	– Dutch-raised white and lilac, well formed for show
Esau	– a new yellow from Holland
Evelyn Rumbold	– purple, popular for show
Franklyn Festival	– new British giant, bronze hues
Fujoh	– a good white from Japan
Go American	– bronze, top-ranking show giant
Hamari Girl	– perhaps the best British giant ever raised, pink
H.M. Queen Elizabeth	– yellow, a veteran now, but still good
Holland Festival	– orange and white bicolour, one of the best
Inca Rearguard	– raised recently, a well-formed pink-white, British
Je Maintiendrai	– light bronze on good stems
Jocondo	– best purple for show, from Holland
Kidd's Climax	– still one of the very best, pink and yellow from New Zealand
Lavender Perfection	– another veteran, but the name holds true
Lavengro	– fine British dahlia, deep lavender
Liberator	– red, formationally perfect, Australian
Lula Pattie	– white, possibly the biggest dahlia we have, from the USA
Margaret Duross	– American bronze popular for show work
Nancy Markow	– an Australian newcomer, good form, yellow

Night Editor	– deep purple, excellent on the show bench, from the USA
Penn's Gift	– massive lilac giant from Pennsylvania,
Pink Master	– sport of the famous 'The Master'
Playboy	– a 1973 arrival, pale yellow, British cup winner

Decorative Dahlias

Sorachi No Aki	– from Japan, red, bronze and yellow, attractive
The Master	– bronze, a fine show dahlia
Trelawny	– Cornish-raised bronze and red, excellent for show

Uchuu	– a really big red giant from Japan
Wise Guy	– a good red from Holland

LARGE-FLOWERED DECORATIVES (8–10 in. in diameter)

Alden Classic	– a good dark pink from Australia
Ballegovation	– orange, well-formed, from Holland
Blithe Spirit	– bright red, tipped white
Cover Girl	– another bicolour, lilac and white
Croydon Dignity	– an Australian red of note
Croydon Snotop	– a veteran dahlia, white and easy to grow
Ed Lloyd	– named after a famous American dahlia-man, pink and good
Enfield Salmon	– colour as name, a top show variety
Lynette Hawton	– delicate shades of pink and white, Australian
Mascot	– another good Australian, orange and white bicolour
Moon Probe	– blends of yellow and orange, from Holland
Mrs McDonald Quill	– New Zealand red and white bicolour
Polly Bergen	– lilac-pink touched with gold, a beauty
Polyand	– an Australian lavender, a top show variety
President Kennedy	– deep red, good form, from Holland
Robert Damp	– yellow touched with bronze, excellent for show
San Luis Rey	– lavender-pink, good form, from Holland
Shirley Jane	– yellow and bronze, one of the very best
Silver City	– white, possibly the best we have today, British
Vacation	– a good bronze for garden and show work, from Holland
Velvet Trophy	– another good Dutch raising, velvety-red on good stems

MEDIUM-FLOWERED DECORATIVES (6–8 in. in diameter)

Actress	– varying shades of red, from Holland
Arc de Triomphe	– a veteran bronze, and Dutch, despite its name

Ballego's Glory	– attractive reds and yellows in this beauty
Barbara Rooke	– bronze sport of famous 'Terpo'
Betty Russell	– the yellow sport of 'Barbara Rooke'
Borddin	– new arrival from Holland, orange and yellow blends
Breckland Joy	– bronze, one of the famous show mediums
Charles Ondries	– lilac, from Australia
Chombu	– one of the best whites, Dutch
Clyde	– a good show pink from Australia
Crossfield Delight	– yellow and white bicolour
Curly White	– an unusual informal medium, colour as name, from Holland
Daleko National	– a new arrival, British, lilac and full of potential
Decora	– a good clear yellow from Holland
Deuil du Roi Albert	– purple and white, a veteran still going strong
Deutschland	– one of the best reds
Duet	– dark red, tipped white, a good one from the USA
Evelyn Foster	– good new trials winner from the USA, white
First Lady	– California's fine medium, one of the best, yellow
Foxfire	– a British-raised formal medium, darkest purple-red
Frau Annie Anders	– a veteran but prolific orange
Gentle Hint	– delicate shades of pink and white, a beauty
Golden Hit	– orange blends, Dutch
Golden Turban	– long-stemmed, orange, a show medium
Hamari Approval	– bronze, yellow and pink in this British show medium
Hamari Boldness	– one of the best reds, for all purposes
Hellas	– Dutch, white, and excellent in all respects
High Adventure	– A pale orange, good for show
House of Orange	– one of Holland's famous 'oldies', still a good dahlia
Inca Galaxy	– Inca dahlias are British, this is a good show yellow
Jan Teulings	– from Holland as the name implies, a flame

Jersey Beauty	– this pink dahlia has been around a long time, still good
Kismet	– a show bronze from Germany
Knightsbridge	– a very good variety from Holland, orange blends
Lady Isabella	– from Australia, a good white
Lilac Time	– colour as name, a very easy grower
Majuba	– very popular as a garden medium, dark purple-red
Marble Arch	– white, with show form, Dutch
Mexicana	– scarlet and gold, one of the most colourful mediums
Mother of Pearl	– attractive colour of white and lilac flush
Mrs A. Woods	– excellent show medium, lavender-pink
New Country	– glowing orange-bronze, for show or garden
Oranjeklant	– bright orange and yellow, an eyecatcher
Palomar Snotop	– a very good white from the USA
Pattern	– lilac with white tipping, a real beauty
Peace	– one of the very best whites
Perran Sylvia	– British-raised yellow, for all purposes
Perran White	– prolific white, from the same raiser
Pink Brecland Joy	– pink sport of 'Breckland Joy', ideal for show work
Regal Choice	– deep purple, good form
Rendezvous	– tall-growing bronze
Rosella	– rich pink, lovely, Dutch
Showman's Delight	– orange and yellow, and of course good for show
Snowstorm	– a real veteran, white and very popular
Sterling Silver	– tall-growing white, excellent for show
Tartan	– this Australian purple and white is excellent for garden work
Tenderly	– new show medium, orange-buff
Terpo	– one of the most famous mediums, red and show-worthy
Thames Valley	– this yellow Dutch raising is new and promising
Winning Hit	– deep red on good stems, a garden medium
Worton Twyn	– British raised, a well-formed orange
Yes Sir!	– pink with some white, show potential
Young Bess	– despite its name, a real veteran, dark pink

SMALL-FLOWERED DECORATIVES (4–6 in. in diameter)

Amethyst	– near-blue, good for cut-flower work
Angel Face	– popular red and white bicolour
Arabian Night	– black-red, a grand addition to any collection
Austin	– a yellow, heavily-built
Best Wishes	– yellow, excellent form, for show
Biddenham Fire	– flame, a British-raised beauty
Bokay	– water-lily form, dark pink and prolific
Bouncer	– well-formed pink and white from Holland
Buttercrunch	– yellow garden dahlia, very new
Cherry Wine	– colour as name, raised in England
Chinese Lantern	– orange-red and yellow, a great little dahlia
Christine Hall	– well-formed lilac for show and garden
Crossfield Champion	– a good deep red from the North
Declaration	– from Holland, a bright red for show
Dedham	– shades of white and lavender, excellent for exhibition
Delectus	– white, water-lily form
Disneyland	– red, yellow and bronze in this attractive cut flower
Edinburgh	– purple with white tips, old but reliable
El Cid	– from Holland, a yellow water-lily
Fête d'Orange	– trials winner, colour as name, excellent
Flutterby	– British raised, red and yellow bicolour
Frank Hornsey	– For show, orange and yellow blends
Glorie Van Heemstede	– yellow, water-lily form, a veteran of quality
Gerrie Hoek	– perhaps the most famous cut flower, pink and profuse
Golden Leader	– bright orange, plenty of bloom all season
Hadrian's Gold	– a well-built, orange, for all purposes
Hallwood Dandy	– light bronze, reflexing, excellent for show
Hamari Fiesta	– red and yellow, a real cracker and a personal favourite
Haseley Delight	– lilac, plenty of bloom, reliable
Helly Boudewijn	– the famous Dutch white, everybody's favourite
Inca Dusk	– rich purple, good form, for show
Ivor's Choice	– dark red with show possibilities
Jacamar	– a new yellow overlaid with lilac, a great combination

Jane Wareham	– from Sussex, a reliable red cut flower
Jescot Jim	– dear old 'Jim', bright yellow
Joan Collins	– from Durham, a yellow that does well
Lady Dorothy	– a new red on strong stems for show work
Lady Tweedsmuir	– a well-formed lilac from Scotland
Lure	– an unusual purple-red, plenty of bloom
Marie Rust	– popular with showmen, deep orange
Mary Richards	– a famous show small decorative, pink and white
Master Robert	– yellow and purple blends, top trials winner
Meiro	– unusual bluish hue, Japanese
Mrs K. Hadow	– raised in Northern Ireland, yellow and orange blends
Neil Lewis	– dark pink and bronze blend in this show small
Never Before	– a grand flame from Holland, well-formed for show
Orchid Lilac	– lilac and white, a lovely flower for all purposes
Paris	– a newcomer in lilac for the exhibitor
Philip Sant	– a good yellow cut flower
Polly Peachum	– pink and orange a beauty
Prairie Fire	– a real startling colour, flame and yellow suffusions
Puckish	– an almost globular finish to this yellow
Rosemary Webb	– masses of cut blooms with this pink and white
Rothesay Robin	– the sensation of twenty years ago, a pink for show
Scarlet Beauty	– colour as name, water-lily form
Snow Queen	– a globular white, some lavender, for show work
Splashes	– lilac, splashed purple, a lovely dahlia
That's It!	– a top show variety, bright red
Thelma Mitchell	– another good show variety, orange hues
Trendy	– attractive combination of red and yellow
Trunkey	– a good bronze for exhibition
Twiggy	– pink blooms by the score, water-lily form
Vicky Crutchfield	– dark pink blends, water-lily form
White Hunter	– colour as name, a show small decorative
Wootton Huntsman	– very new mid-red for the exhibitor
Worton Gold	– glowing bronze, for show

Worton Superb	– a globular lilac of great potential, garden or show

MINIATURE-FLOWERED DECORATIVES (up to 4 in. in diameter)

Ampère	– a lovely little red, finishes like a ball
Chorus Girl	– lavender-pink, prolific
Colour Magic	– flame and yellow blending for this beauty
Crossfield Crofter	– a good red from Yorkshire
David Howard	– almost black foliage offsets this brilliant orange
Decoy	– red and orange blends, with masses of bloom
Doris Duke	– a very popular miniature decorative, dark pink
Feyencord	– a Dutch bicolour, red and white
Gigi	– attractive purple with white tipping
Gipsy Kiss	– lovely name for a lovely dahlia, lilac hues
Girl Scout	– yellow, easy to grow, for all purposes
Greenacres Robert	– good form, bright red
Horn of Plenty	– a scarlet of note, from Holland
Jean Fairs	– palest buff, scores of blooms, ideal for flower arranging
Jescot Tangerine	– colour as name, bright orange hues
Jo's Choice	– and the showman's choice too, a top red for show
Kochelsee	– a veteran Dutchman, scarlet and going strong!
Lark	– one of the best yellows in this group
Lavendale	– a new British miniature, lilac blends
Lilianne Ballego	– a famous miniature, bronze, from Holland
Murrayfield	– from Scotland, red and yellow blends
Musette	– this red and white bicolour is extremely popular
Newby	– apricot and dark pink in this formal British beauty
Newchurch	– a pink favoured by showmen
Pink Newby	– colour sport of the famous 'Newby'
Rose Newby	– another hue in this famous family
Safe Shot	– orange shades for this miniature
Schweitzer's Kokarde	– red and yellow blends in this German miniature

Virgo	– a white miniature of substance, plenty of bloom
White Nymph	– an excellent white for cutting and garden

13 Pompon Dahlias

Pompon Dahlias came from Germany in the middle of the nineteenth century. They were regarded in those days, evidently, as 'Fancy (or Ball) Dahlias in miniature'. From that time they have increased their popularity and are now much used, as cut flowers and also to give a blaze of colour in the flower border. Some wags have rudely called the Pompon Dahlia the Golf Ball Dahlia, but today there are numerous varieties which are certainly bigger and more beautiful than golf balls!

The official description of Pompon Dahlias is that they have flowers like those of Ball Dahlias, but smaller. There are Large-flowered Pompon Dahlias, Medium-flowered Pompon Dahlias, and Small-flowered Pompon Dahlias. Large-flowered Pompons have flowers over 3 in but not usually exceeding 4 in in diameter. When they do exceed 4 in in diameter they are listed with Ball Dahlias, details of which will be found in Chapter 14.

Pompon Dahlias, and particularly the Small-flowered group, have become extremely popular, not only for the show bench but also as cut flowers and for glorious displays in the garden.

There are well over three hundred varieties of Pompon Dahlias, and it would be impossible in a book like this to list more than a few. Once again, I have had to make a choice, and I hope that these selected will give great pleasure to readers.

Small-flowered Pompon Dahlias

Varieties

Andrew Lockwood	– a perfect pom in all respects, pink
Berin's Willo	– a globular beauty in purple
Gale Lane	– orange and yellow suffusions in this attractive pom
Hall mark	– pink with some lavender in a top-rated show pom
Joe Morris	– dark red with some yellow
Little Conn	– a mid-red that finishes beautifully
Little Willo	– one of the best whites

Mark Willo	– pink colour variations
Minley Marion	– a flame pom from Mr Wilkins
Minley Louise	– bright orange, again from Mr Wilkins
Minley Sharon	– an unusual purple and white mixture
Moorplace	– acknowledged as one of the best poms ever
Noreen	– lavender-pink, from Australia
Pam	– pink and white, also from Australia
Pop Willo	– orange and maize blends
Red Jubilee	– another of the good Australian poms, colour as name
Rhondda	– lavender flushed white, regarded as the best pom
Small World	– Australian again, white flecked purple
Willo's Violet	– a great old timer, still going strong, violent blends

14 Ball Dahlias

These dahlias used to be known as Double Show and Fancy Dahlias, and it is claimed that they form the oldest group of dahlias currently being grown. At one time Show Dahlias were put into a separate group of their own because it was claimed that Fancy Dahlias were always striped or tipped. Today, however, they are grouped together. The flowers are fully doubled and over 4 in. in diameter. They are almost globular, and their centre florets are like the outer ones only smaller. The florets invariably have incurved margins, which are blunt at the mouth, short and tubular.

We need to say a big 'thank-you' to the dahlia breeders in the 1800s, for there are varieties in this group which were raised over eighty years ago and which are still found in gardens and which may easily be winning prizes at local shows. The older generation certainly love this group of dahlias. They like the size of the blooms, and appreciate their perfect regularity. I know many keen gardeners who state with authority that there are no dahlias like the Double Shows introduced sixty years ago.

Varieties

The Ball Dahlia classification, which takes in the erstwhile Double Show and Fancy Dahlias, also embraces, in the Miniature Ball section, a great number of dahlias previously described as large and medium poms.

SMALL BALL (4–6 in. in diameter)

Anneke Weidner	– from Germany, a purple and white beauty
Capulet	– maroon-purple with good form
Davina Rosemary	– deep cherry-red, geometrically perfect
Dottie D	– shades of pink in this American dahlia
Gloire de Lyon	– a veteran white, still obtainable
New Miller	– yellow and white bicolour, British
Mrs Anderson	– a top winner when introduced recently, lavender-pink
Onslow Princess	– best yellow yet raised, perfectly round

Opal	– delicate pink and white, for all purposes
Puff Ball	– another in pastel-pink shades
Purple Globe	– name perfectly describes form and colour
Snowsong	– a British-raised white, grown all over the world
Standard	– chocolate with yellow tips, lovely
Vaguely Noble	– a purple new and very good

MINIATURE BALL (up to 4 in. in diameter)

Blossom	– blossom pink, a good dahlia from Holland
Bull's Eye	– bright red
Betty Armstrong	– a new orange with promise
Connoisseur's Choice	– perfect form, red, excellent for show
Florence Vernon	– a lilac of recent introduction
Globular	– purple and pink, a beauty that was a medium pom before
Golden Fizz	– fizzy is right! a lovely little yellow
Little Willem	– from Holland, a red and white bicolour
Nettie	– undoubtedly the best show miniature, yellow
Rothesay Superb	– a red from Scotland and one of the very best
Worton Joy	– lilac, and a great little dahlia, a personal favourite

'Fascination', a Paeony-flowered variety

15 Miscellaneous Dahlias

Although some people may feel that Collarettes should have a chapter to themselves, I have decided to include them here, together with Anenome-flowered, Paeony-flowered, Star and Single-flowered Dahlias and the Top Mix varieties. I shall start with Collarettes, because the others have few varieties to be listed.

Collarettes

There are three groups of Collarette Dahlias: (a) Singles, which have only a single row of ray florets, one collar and one central disc, (b) Paeony-flowered Collarettes, which have two colours and two or more rows of ray florets plus a central disc, and (c) Decorative Collarette Dahlias which are similar to (b) but Fully Double.

Many people consider Collarettes to be the most beautiful dahlias of all. They are certainly very highly coloured, and, of course, they are striking because the collar is invariably the perfect foil to the outer florets; you will find very many lovely and striking contrasts among the Collarette varieties. Most varieties produce blooms on good strong stems. Whereas ten years ago

'Sincerity', a Collarette variety

Collarette Dahlias

they were not so popular, Collarettes are gradually becoming more so, especially in Holland and France.

With Collarettes it is important to cut the flowers while the blooms are still young, because if you wait until the flowers are fully expanded, the ray florets are apt to drop soon afterwards.

Anemone-flowered Dahlias

Perhaps there is no dahlia which differs more from other types than the Anemone-flowered. It has an outer rim of flattened ray florets surrounding a glorious dense group of tubular florets. These are certainly longer than the disc florets of the Single Dahlias. Curiously enough, it has never been a very popular dahlia in Britain.

Anemone-flowered Dahlias

Orchid-flowered Dahlias

Orchid-flowered Dahlias are smaller, on the whole, than Single Dahlias, and are so called because the sides of the florets roll upwards, thus showing their undersides. Because these differ in colour there is usually a fascinating colour contrast. My friends in France are entranced with these particular varieties, which are also to be seen growing in Canada and the United States, in large numbers. For some reason they are not at all popular in Britain.

I suppose the reason why Orchid-flowered Dahlias have never been popular with growers in Britain is that they are not imposing enough. Some people have suggested that they are rather ragged in their appearance. They do look peculiar. On the other hand many orchids look peculiar, but they are popular and expensive. I have a hunch that now that floral art and indoor decoration with flowers and foliage have become so popular, someone will discover the great value of Orchid-flowered Dahlias.

Paeony-flowered Dahlias

Perhaps the most famous of all Paeony-flowered Dahlias is the 'Bishop of Llandaff', which has the most lovely dark brown-purpley, almost black leaves. The flowers are crimson and it is a variety that is used again and again as a centrepiece for a dahlia bed in parks. Paeony-flowered Dahlias have blooms consisting of two or more rows of more or less flattened ray florets and a central disc.

Many people seem to think that this group of dahlias is the Cinderella of dahlias. They are not supposed to have any particular perfection of form, nor are their 'habits' said to be good. You seldom see them in gardens today.

Paeony-flowered Dahlias

Single Dahlias

Single Dahlias have a single outer ring of ray florets. These are broad and overlapping, and the centre is an attractive disc. There are two main types: (a) Show Singles, which have smooth ray florets forming a perfectly round flower, the petals being broad and overlapping; and (b) Singles, which have ray florets

Single Dahlias

overlapping to a lesser extent, so that the tips of the petals are invariably separated. Show Singles are difficult to find in Britain today.

Star Dahlias

This is a very small group, and varieties are rarely found in this country. My grandmother, who was a very keen gardener, loved Star Dahlias because they were excellent as cut flowers, and most unusual and attractive when grown in the garden. The blooms are quite small and slightly cup-shaped. Around the central disc there are two or three rows of gently pointed ray florets. These florets overlap a little at their more or less recurved margins which, of course, gives the flowers a star-like appearance.

I would be grateful to know of any readers who are still growing Star Dahlias today.

Topmix

These are the tiniest of all dahlias, just an inch across on low-growing bushes. They may be used in pots or tubs, as border plants or even as house plants.

Varieties

Andrie's Wonder – bronze, yellow and purple blends in this

	dahlia which assumes the form of a chrysanthemum
Asahi Chohje	– a red and white bicolour from Japan, paeony form
Comet	– a deep red dahlia from Australia, anemone form
Giraffe	– the famous orchid form of the dahlia, yellow and bronze hues with spotted petals
Holcombe	– pink and orange, orchid form
Honey	– pink and yellow, anemone form
Janome Chohje	– another Japanese dahlia, in red and yellow, anemone form
Japanese Octopus	– a novelty of twirling yellow petals
Kuroi Hitomi	– a deep red dahlia with the form of a rose
New Galah	– lilac blends in this orchid-flowered variety
Pink Giraffe	– pink sport of the famous 'Giraffe'
Scarlet Comet	– sport of the Australian 'Comet', 'anemone' form
White Orchid	– a single dahlia, colour and form as name

Topmix

Chessy	– a bronze-yellow
Exotic Dwarf	– pink and purple, one of the best
Facet	– deep orange-bronze
Inflammable	– red and flame blends, as the name suggests
Little Drummer Boy	– a perfect name for a perfect red mini-dahlia
Petit Michel	– a host of bright purple blooms
Red Dwarf	– two shades of red in attractive rings
White Lilliput	– a white, recommended in this form

16 Pests and diseases

Insects

Dahlias, unfortunately, have no special immunity from pests and diseases. There are insect pests which attack the stems, the branches, the shoots, the leaves, the buds, the flowers, and also the underground tubers. Many of them have different stages of development and so it is necessary to learn something of their life histories, habits, and methods of feeding. Once one knows these facts one can learn to apply the right control methods.

Some insects, such as aphids (or greenflies) have sucking mouth parts. They push their proboscis or trunk right through the upper epidermis into the centre of the leaves or stems so that they can suck the sap from the inside. While doing so, they cannot help pushing some of their saliva in at the same time. This may well be infected with virus diseases and so these insects are called vectors. (Vectors are insects which cause the infection of plants with such diseases.) It is necessary to combat such pests with what may be called a 'paralyzing agent', such as nicotine.

Other insects have biting mouth parts with which they actually eat the leaves or stems. These will be caterpillars of various sizes and kinds and certain kinds of beetles. Since they eat the leaves the best way to kill these pests is to dust the foliage with a poison. There are dangers, however, in using arsenical powders or sprays, and many people prefer to use instead liquid derris, or liquid pyrethrum.

In addition, there are insect pests like wireworms and cutworms which attack the plants below soil level, slugs and snails which will eat the stems and leaves, and which can be a great nuisance to dahlias soon after they are planted, and creatures like earwigs and red spiders which require particular methods of control.

Fungus Diseases

Fungus diseases are caused by lowly little plants which live on the stems, leaves and flowers of other plants. Typical fungus diseases found in dahlias are: mildew, rust, smut, and black spot. The spores of a fungus blow about in the wind and then drop down on to the leaves from above. If the gardener sprays the leaf of a plant with a suitable fungicide before it is attacked, then when the minute spore lands it is killed immediately. It is far easier to prevent a fungus attack than it is to control one after it has actually caught hold. Once the fungus has sent out its little 'roots' into the leaves, i.e. between the upper and lower epidermis, there is no way of reaching this part of the trouble.

Precautions

As may be imagined, the obvious prevention is to grow the plants as healthily as possible. Dahlias growing in properly manured, well-drained land never suffer as badly as plants put out into water-logged ground, or ground that has not been properly prepared or fed, and lacks humus. It is always necessary to hoe regularly among the plants in the early stages of growth, and if this is done shallowly with a Dutch hoe it will reduce the infestations of surface caterpillars, wireworms, and the grubs of cockchafer beetles. If weeds are kept down, capsid bugs, cutworms and wireworms are discouraged, as are many species of aphids which depend on wild plants for the completion of their life cycle.

It is most important, also, to compost all vegetable refuse and never to allow it to lie about uselessly, since many pests breed among rubbish and in rubbish heaps. The bases of hedges, where pests may lurk and breed, should also be cleaned out, and broken bricks, old flower pots, and clinkers should never be allowed to remain in heaps, for it is in such places that slugs and snails and woodlice are found harbouring.

Burn decaying tree stumps to prevent them from encouraging woodlice, or paint them with a strong hormone, known by its formula as 2:5D and sold on the market as SBK.

Be careful to follow the instructions in Chapter 4 with regard to the manuring of the soil. Remember that if overdoses of nitrogen are given the plants will tend to be soft and sappy, and they are then more susceptible to both pests and diseases. Sometimes, of course, a dahlia grower suffers because a neighbour makes no attempt at all to control diseases and pests, and I know at least one man who takes the trouble, when spraying his own plants, to treat those of his neighbours at the same time.

There are no particular precautions to be taken against

fungus diseases, other than the early spraying of fungicides. The same general recommendations apply as for prevention of insect attacks: start with healthy stock, prepare and manure the ground properly, give the plants plenty of room for development and, by means of hoeing, mulching and watering, keep the plants growing well the whole time.

Lastly, be very careful from whom you purchase your dahlia plants. It is never wise to take advantage of cheap offers from unknown nurserymen or from hucksters who may knock on your door. It is so easy to introduce serious virus diseases with poorly-grown plants, so do beware. Buy healthy, sturdy plants of known varieties, from reliable nurserymen who are known to be members of the British Dahlia Growers' Association.

The pressure sprayer is a most useful addition to your garden armoury

Sprayers and Dusters

The kinds you choose will depend on the size of your garden, and whether you have £10 or £40 to spend on spray machinery. A nurseryman who is growing dahlias on a large scale will of course have a high-powered spraying machine, so that he can get over all the ground in a short space of time. On the other hand, the gardener with just a few dahlias may only need a good syringe and a hand duster in order to get efficient control of pests and diseases.

For the normal garden I would recommend the Solo sprayer, which costs about £3.* It has a double-action pump which ensures that the spray jet is being emitted all the time. It is attached to a rubber hose and filter so that the nozzle doesn't get

* Prices change under modern conditions

blocked. All you have to do is to mix the fungicide or insecticide in a bucket, put in the end of the rubber hose, and pump away. This handy sprayer has in its nozzle a mistifier which can easily be unscrewed. Remove it and you can send a jet of 15 ft or so, put it back and then the spray will be a very wide cone of fine drops.

As for dusting machines, one can buy these in various sizes, or one can buy what are called 'Dust Guns', which are considerably dearer.

There are, of course, knapsack sprayers for those with fairly large gardens, as well as knapsack dusters for those who prefer to use dusts instead of sprays. The advantage of using dusts is that of course you are not carting a lot of water about, but sprays undoubtedly give better control. Yet dusts may be used with good effect, especially if they are applied with a 'gun' which makes certain that the fungicidal or insecticidal dust travels widely over an area. I prefer to use a rotary fan dust gun.

In the greenhouse one can use fumigants, and most horticultural manufacturers today produce smoke bombs or generators which produce the necessary type of fumigant for the pest or disease concerned.

Insecticides

To be effective insecticides must be accompanied by a suitable wetting or spreading agent. Sometimes the manufacturer includes the spreader with the insecticide, but when a pure killer like nicotine is purchased the gardener has to add the spreader himself. Insects must be thoroughly wetted if they are to be killed, and the plants should be given a thorough drenching. When applying the jet of spray see that it reaches the undersides of the leaves as well as the upper surface. Spraying is best done on a warm, sunny day.

Nicotine is a widely-used insecticide. It is often used as a spray for fear that as a dust it might blow into other gardens nearby and perhaps cause trouble. The usual formula is $\frac{1}{4}$ oz liquid nicotine and $\frac{1}{4}$ lb soft soap to $2\frac{1}{2}$ gallons of water.

Liquid derris has given me the best results. It is excellent for controlling young caterpillars, aphids and red spider. Its great advantage is that it is non-poisonous to human beings or animals, and so can safely be kept in the potting shed. It must not, however, be used near a garden pool for it can kill fish. If bought as a liquid it should be diluted with water in accordance with the manufacturer's instructions on the container. If bought as a powder to mix with water for spraying, it is usual to use $\frac{1}{4}$ lb Derris in 12 gallons of water. The manufacturer usually adds a 'wetter', or 'spreader' to his preparation, so that all the gardener has to do is to stir the Derris powder into a little water first, so as to make a paste, then add the rest of the water to complete the formula.

Derris dust is much used, with great success. Some firms make a special derris dust with a high Rotonone content, which is recommended. It should be stored in a sealed container and used while still fresh. A good derris dust will be light, with extremely small particles, so that it can be evenly distributed all over the plants without causing them any disfigurement.

Fungicides

In the past there were two main types of fungicide, based on sulphur and copper. (Recipes for these fungicides are given below.) Latterly, two new types of fungicides have been introduced: Captan and Karathane. The latter gives excellent results against mildew. I have found them clean and easy to handle, and neither leaves unsightly deposits on the stems, foliage or flowers. They should be used in accordance with the instructions on the containers.

Bordeaux mixture $1\frac{1}{2}$ lb hydrated lime and 1 lb finely powdered copper sulphate to 10 gallons of water. Dissolve the crystals of finely powdered copper sulphate overnight in a wooden, china or enamel container. Pour this solution carefully into the lime and water solution you will have already made in the morning, stirring all the time.

A metal vessel should never be used with Bordeaux mixture because of the risk of corrosion.

Burgundy mixture 4 oz finely powdered copper sulphate and 5 oz washing soda to $2\frac{1}{2}$ gallons of water. Dissolve the copper sulphate overnight in 1 gallon of water, and the washing soda overnight in $1\frac{1}{2}$ gallons of water. Pour the washing soda solution slowly into the copper sulphate solution, stirring all the time. Keep agitated and use at once. Always use wooden or enamel vessels, as in the case of Bordeaux mixture.

Liver of sulphur $1\frac{1}{4}$ oz liver of sulphur and 1 tablespoonful of a liquid detergent like Stergene to $2\frac{1}{2}$ gallons of water. Stir well and use immediately.

Colloidal sulphur has been described as 'liquid sulphur' in a very finely divided state. Dissolve in water as advised on the bottle in which the colloidal sulphur is supplied.

Colloidal copper may be described as 'liquid Bordeaux' in a finely divided state. It is dissolved in water in accordance with the instructions given on the label on the bottle.

Poison Baits

There are some pests that are best controlled by using baits. The pest is encouraged to come and eat the bait provided, and the special poison that has been mixed with the bait then causes certain death. Some of the poisons used are arsenical and must be applied with care.

Nippon is a famous Japanese remedy which will kill ants in their nests without a trace. It can be applied wherever ants give trouble.

Bran and Paris green is a poisonous mixture used for the control of leather-jackets. The formula is as follows: 10 lb bran and $\frac{1}{2}$ lb Paris green to $\frac{1}{2}$ gallon of water. The bran should be damped with the water, and the Paris green stirred in so that each part of the bran is covered with this green arsenical poison. The mixture should be applied all over the surface of the ground in the evening, a further application being given the following evening should it rain overnight. The quantity given above is sufficient to cover half an acre. This is basically Arsenic and should never be used unless absolutely necessary.

Greenhouse fumigants

From a horticultural chemist one can buy smoke 'bombs' or pellets which, when ignited, will produce a 'fog' penetrating every part of the greenhouse. These fogs or smokes give a high degree of control over most insect pests, including aphids, capsid bugs, thrips, white fly, leaf miner, red spiders and caterpillars. There are also smoke pellets that will produce a fungicidal smoke. There is no quicker or better way of controlling pests and diseases in a greenhouse than by means of one of these modern fumigants.

Insect Pests

Ants

Ants do two things: they make nests in the soil, making it difficult for the dahlia tubers to develop as they should, and they clamber up the plants, carrying aphids with them because their great desire is to establish aphid colonies. They love the honeydew which the cornicles of the aphids exude. Having established colonies on as many plants as possible, they come regularly to 'milk' the aphids.

Control Get rid of them by using the Japanese insecticide called Nippon. It also helps to dust around the base of the dahlias with a derris dust; this will discourage the ants, and earwigs too.

Aphids

It is important to try and control all aphids because these are the main creatures to spread virus diseases. There are several different kinds of aphids that may be seen on dahlia plants; they are commonly classified as 'greenflies' and 'blackflies'. They suck the leaves and stems, they cause the foliage to curl, and they may distort the growth of the plants. With severe attacks, dahlias become stunted in growth. Aphids may be found on young plants in the greenhouse as well as on older dahlias out of doors.

Control Most keen growers take the precaution of dipping the dahlia plants in a solution of nicotine and water before setting them out in open ground. This dipping in a bucket of nicotine insecticide only takes a second or so, but it is of course most effective. Once a fortnight, after this, it is well worth spraying with liquid derris. The plants should be thoroughly soaked on each occasion and the undersides of the leaves be treated as carefully as the upper surfaces.

If the plants are sprayed regularly during the first two months after planting, there is seldom any further trouble.

Capsid Bugs

These small brownish-green or green insects are suckers, just like the aphids. The brownish-green type is often known as the Tarnished Plant Bug, or the Bishop Bug because it has a shape rather like the mitre of a bishop. Adult capsids are $\frac{1}{4}$in. long while the larvae are even smaller. They are often difficult to find because as the gardener approaches the plant the creatures promptly drop to the ground. When they are older they quickly fly away or they rush and seek cover underneath the leaves.

They are very swift-moving.

But it is possible to notice the puncture they make on the leaves. The trouble is usually first seen on dahlias late in June and early in July and further attacks may develop during August and September, the work of the next generation. Gardeners sometimes fail to notice the trouble until too late, for when the damage is really serious the bugs may easily have moved on to another host.

Control It is important to anticipate an attack by spraying dahlias about the third week in June, using liquid derris. The ground too should be soaked with the wash because so many of the capsids will fall onto the soil during the spraying operation.

Do not confuse the punctures made by earwigs with those made by capsids. The holes of the former are much more clean-cut, with the result that there is far less distortion.

Caterpillars

There are a number of different kinds of caterpillars which may attack dahlias, those, for instance, of the Angle Shades Moth, the Swift Moth, and the Tortrix Moth. When the caterpillars are young and small they are much less easy to detect, but the damage they do is usually fairly obvious. The caterpillar of the Swift Moth will attack the tubers, and to prevent this a derris powder may be raked into the soil. Some caterpillars will feed inside the stems of the dahlias, and cause the branches or stems to collapse as a result. The only thing to do, in this case, is to cut off the stem, find the caterpillar culprit and kill it. I have seldom seen stem-boring caterpillars at work in this country, so readers need not be apprehensive. It can, however, give a great deal of trouble in Canada and the USA.

Control The ordinary caterpillar eats the leaves and the young stems and can easily be killed by using liquid derris in the early stages. This, when diluted, is sprayed all over the plants with as much force as possible.

Cuckoo Spit

There is no difficulty at all in recognizing an attack of the nymph of the froghopper, for this looks like spittle on the stems or leaves. If the froth is parted and examined a grey-brown creature, $\frac{1}{4}$in. long, will be found underneath. Alternatively, if it is still in the nymph stage it will be a pale yellowy-green. Actually these froghoppers do very little harm, but they do make the plants look unsightly.

Control It is a simple matter to hand pick the plants and destroy the pests under the spittle, or, if the trouble is extensive, the plants may be sprayed with liquid derris. In this case, however, the wash must be applied with force as it is necessary to get through the froth to the pest below.

Cutworms

These are really dirty-grey or brown caterpillars which creep about on the surface of the soil or just below. They nibble the stems of the dahlias, either just below or just above the ground level, making a complete girdle. The attacked plants wilt and finally snap off at the point where the nibbling has taken place. During the day these pests usually hide away under leaves, stones, or clods of earth.

Control A sharp look-out should be kept for these caterpillars; if you are really observant you can find them in the day-time. Derris dust may be put around the base of the plants, and then lightly hoed in.

Earwigs

For some reason the one pest of dahlias that everybody talks about is the earwig. This I think is because children invariably find earwigs in the large blooms, and the stories told them by grown-ups about the danger of these insects in their ears always frighten them. In fact, in well-cultivated gardens, earwigs are seldom seen.

They nibble the petals of the blooms and cut holes in the leaves. These holes are beautifully cut, quite different from the damage done by capsid bugs.

Control The old-fashioned method of control is to fill 3-in. pots with straw or wood wool and put them upside down on the tops of the bamboos or stakes supporting the plants. The earwigs then hide in the pots. If the pots are taken off first thing in the morning, and two fingers are put over the straw wood wool to keep it in place, it is quite easy to knock the earwigs out into a tin or bucket containing a little paraffin, where they will be killed

with derris. The earwigs will easily drop to the ground while the dusting operation is being carried out, so treat the soil with derris dust also.

Earwigs can be trapped in upturned pots filled with straw. Empty the captives into a paraffin-filled tin each morning

Red Spiders

The name 'red spider' is unfortunate, because, first of all, the creatures are not spiders but mites, and secondly, they are not red but usually straw-coloured. You seldom get serious trouble with red spiders in this country, but it is a very serious pest in parts of the United States and South Africa. It always delights in dryness and never flourishes where the leaves are regularly syringed with water.

You will find the mites on the under side of the leaves if you look for them with a magnifying glass. They are only 1/60 in. long, and they usually cluster together in minute white webs. The leaves, which are normally dark green, turn yellow after an attack and in very bad cases go dark brown.

Control Do *not* attempt to control red spiders by the use of BHC or DDT, because these will kill the normal predators that feed on them, and cause the spiders to increase alarmingly. Liquid derris is ideal for controlling red spiders.

People who are growing dahlias under glass may have quite serious attacks of red spiders because these spiders revel in the extra warmth provided. They live in the woodwork from season to season, and so it is always worth while to scrub down the inside of the house with strong liquid derris when the house is vacant. Some nurserymen use Azo Benzene fumigants with success. They light the bombs in the evening after the house has been shut down and then open the doors and ventilators very early in the morning to let out the spent fumes.

Slugs

Slugs and snails used to be a problem, especially in the early stages of dahlias, but since the introduction of sedge peat mulchings, there has been very little difficulty.

Control One can buy Draza blue pellets. A strong Pyrethrum liquid can be watered on to the ground where the dahlias are to be planted a few days beforehand and any slugs that may be lurking about will be killed. Once the plants are in the ground it is a simple matter to sprinkle Draza pellets on the top of the soil. These act as a perfect bait. The slugs much prefer the pellets to the dahlias, and are killed immediately they eat them.*

If you take over a town garden where slugs have been breeding for a long time you should adopt the copper sulphate and hydrated lime method. Mix ½ lb of each of these together and then apply the mixture all over the ground, at the rate of 1 oz to the square yard, and fork it into the soil. A second similar dressing may be applied fifteen days before setting out the dahlias. Never apply more than this because an overdose of copper sulphate may poison the soil.

If you think that slugs are coming from the garden next door and there is no complete barrier, such as a wall, between you and your neighbour, then make up the copper sulphate and hydrated lime mixture and sprinkle it along at the base of the

* Birds may eat blue pellets

hedge or wooden fence. This will prevent the passage of slugs from the garden next door to your own ground.

Thrips

These are tiny little black creatures which, under a magnifying glass, always look to me like microscopic crocodiles. The adults are black or dark brown, and the youngsters or larvae a yellowy colour. To discover whether thrips are present I lay a clean white handkerchief on one hand and tap the leaves of the dahlia or an open flower with the other. When thrips are there they will drop on to the white linen when suddenly disturbed, and then you can see them as minute black specks.

It is very important to know whether thrips are giving trouble or not because, like aphids, they can be the vectors of some virus diseases. One of the most serious of these is known as Spotted Wilt. Thrips will also damage the petals, causing tiny white spots to appear.

Control I find that nicotine gives me the best control of thrips. Use it on a nice warm day, preferably at about 11 o'clock. Pure liquid nicotine is obtainable from the chemist, and $\frac{1}{4}$oz of this is sufficient for a $2\frac{1}{2}$ gallon bucketful of water, to which a tablespoonful of liquid detergent has been added. A second spraying with this insecticide should be given after five days, and a third one five days after that.

Wasps

It is curious, the way wasps go for dahlias, but there is no doubt that they attack the stems. Experts tell me that they nibble away the outer 'bark' in order to obtain some material with which to build their nests. They often make quite large wounds, for once they start nibbling at a particular spot they seem to keep on at it. It is said that there are a few varieties of dahlia whioh have a higher sugar content in the sap than others. Wasps go for this sweet sap as well as for nest material.

Control The first thing to do is to try and locate the nest or nests, and then to put a handful of dry derris dust over the top. The wasps take this down with them as they worm their way down the hole and so the larvae below are also killed. Secondly, one can fill 2lb jam jars a quarter full with sugary water, cider and sugar or beer and sugar. Cover the jars with paper and then make a hole in the centre with a pointed pencil. The wasps will find their way in through the hole but will seldom if ever get out.

I have not yet found a way of preventing wasps from coming back repeatedly to the same spot on a dahlia stem. You can dust with derris but they seem not to be deterred. So, to protect stems from further attacks I usually cover the place where the original incision has been made with a small piece of adhesive plaster or insulating tape.

There are very large wasps known as hornets which can also give trouble, but they do not seem to return to the same spot time and time again as do wasps. Frankly, hornets always frighten me, because they are so large and bad-tempered, and if I see them among dahlias I try to 'shoot them down' with one of the aerosols we use for killing flies in the house.

Wireworms

Wireworms are the larvae of the Click Beetle, the most widely distributed of all the soil pests. The Click Beetle is so called because when it is put on its back it can jump vertically into the air to right itself, making a clicking noise at the same time. The beetles will be seen flying about in the sun during the months of May and June. The eggs are laid in grass, either singly or in clusters, during the months of June and July. Please note, therefore, that wireworms invariably start their life in turf. They have three pairs of short legs situated on the first three segments of their bodies, which are brownish-yellow in colour. They are very wiry (hence the name), and so difficult to kill by squeezing between the fingers.

Control Great care should be taken when purchasing turf for greenhouses or frames not to introduce wireworms and so start the trouble in the garden. If wireworms are known to be present in soil, Gammexane should be applied at the rate of $\frac{1}{2}$oz to the square yard, a few days before the dahlias are put out. Gardeners who, like myself, dislike using a chemical of this kind can trap wireworms by spitting small pieces of carrot or potato on the end of a stick, and burying them 2 in. deep in the ground. When these traps are removed at weekly intervals, the wireworms can be picked out and killed in a small tin of paraffin.

Woodlice

These grey creatures have been given all kinds of names: sow bugs, monkey bugs, pea bugs, slaters, and so on. They roll themselves up into little balls when touched. They can give a lot of trouble in the storehouse, where they will attack the tubers and nibble the dormant buds. Even when the plants are out growing in the open ground they can attack the stems at ground level.

Control Fortunately, they are easily controlled by derris dust. Apply this among the tubers in the store shed, if necessary, and use the dust around the plants after they have been growing a week or so.

Be sure to clean up any unsightly clumps in the garden where these creatures may breed. Sometimes in an old garden they collect and hide at the bases of edging tiles or at the bottoms of fences and hedges. Derris dust may be used all over these areas to destroy the creatures.

Fungus Diseases

Crown Call

When this disease attacks dahlias, large black growths resembling cauliflowers in shape appear at the roots and at the base of the stalk of the plants. These peculiarly shaped, cankerous growths ruin the plants in the long run. The trouble is due to a bacteria called *Bacterium tumefaciens.* This will attack plants other than dahlias.

Control Any dahlias found so affected should be dug up and burnt immediately, for there is no known cure. The soil where the plants are growing should be sterilized by heat, if it is going to be used again. If it cannot be so sterilized then it is better not to grow dahlias on that plot of land for some seven or eight years. Buy in new clean stock and plant in another part of the garden.

Dahlia Smut

This disease, *Entyloma dahliae,* was originally called Leaf Spot. Light yellowy green round spots are seen on the leaves at first, and these subsequently turn greyish brown, first of all in the middle and then all over. Eventually the edges of the spots turn dark, and later on the tissue in the centre dies – becomes dry and brittle – and may drop out, so that the leaves appear perforated. Fungus spores blow about during growth, from leaf to leaf and from plant to plant. The fungus will over-winter on any dead leaves which may have inadvertently been stored with the tubers, or on the stumps of the plants themselves, above the tubers.

In the summer the trouble usually appears in late August, but

I have known young plants to be affected in June. Damp weather and damp situations undoubtedly favour the trouble. Some people say that the disease may over-winter in the soil, and that it therefore pays to alter the site of dahlias each season. Acid soils favour the disease, and therefore it is a good thing to apply hydrated lime over the surface of the ground at 3 or 4 oz to the square yard if the trouble is known to be about in the district.

I have found that dahlias planted out early are less liable to be attacked than those planted out late. Cactus Dahlias are certainly very susceptible, but, in my garden at least, Pompon Dahlias are almost immune. Dahlias planted in open sunny situations are never as badly affected as those planted in secluded sheltered spots.

Control The disease can be controlled by spraying with a Bordeaux mixture, which can be bought as a paste ready for mixing with water. Colloidal copper, sold as Bouisol, can be used instead, if desired; it has the advantage of not leaving so many stains. The organic fungicide Captan gives very good results and is well worth trying.

Dahlia Wilt

This disease, which causes a wilt of the dahlias, is a Verticillium. It causes the plants to bear very few flowers indeed. Badly affected dahlias hang their leaves as if there was insufficient moisture in the soil. It is said to be the same fungus that affects the raspberry, and in this case the disease is known as Blue Striped Wilt. It is never advisable, therefore, to grow dahlias near raspberries, and if there are raspberry canes badly affected with this disease it is always better to grub them up and burn them.

Control The only known method of controlling this Verticillium trouble in dahlias is to dig the affected parts up and burn them.

Dry Rot

This disease is probably a Fusarium, and it is claimed by mycologists that unsuitable storage places, which keep the air too dry, may account for the trouble in the tubers.

Control Dig the tubers up after the first frost, and store them in an airy cool place. Stand the tuber clusters upside down for several days so that any moisture in the stems of the stalks may run out. Then store the tubers the right way up. If the disease appears regularly it will be advisable to dust the tubers with a mixture of hydrated lime and flowers of sulphur in equal parts.

Storage sheds and rooms should be cleaned out really thoroughly, after storing, in the spring, and then disinfected. To do this spray the walls, floors, shelving and so on with a 2 per cent solution of formaldehyde. Care has to be taken not to breathe in too much of this spray, and for this reason some gardeners use an old-fashioned gas mask when applying the formalin.

Non-tubering

This is a very curious physiological trouble which has been affecting dahlias recently. When planted the dahlias only produce fibrous roots instead of tubers. The result is that the gardener cannot propagate from the plants and has to buy new dahlias every year from the nursery. It is said that there is some genetical cause for this; it takes place, as a rule, with a number of new varieties. Curiously enough, even those varieties that are said to be bad at tuber production behave differently from season to season.

Control It does help to encourage tuber production if the plants are given plenty of water during a dry summer.

Virus Diseases

By far the most serious trouble met with in dahlia growing is virus disease. In his book, *Beyond the Microscope*, Dr Kenneth Smith states that no one has ever succeeded in growing viruses or causing them to multiply upon an artificial medium of any sort in a laboratory. He calls them 'obligate parasites' which means that viruses are incapable of existing independently. A virus is an extremely minute 'disease' agent which can only be seen with the aid of a special microscope, and which can only multiply when inside a living cell.

Viruses in plants are usually transmitted by thrips or aphids. There is one aphid, in fact, known as *Aphis myzus persicae*, which transmits no fewer than twenty-two different plant viruses. It is possible for a disease to travel from zinnias to asters, from asters to chrysanthemums and from chrysanthemums to dahlias, to mention but a few of the flowering plants. Viruses that affect dahlias will also, of course, attack tomatoes, cucumbers, potatoes and so on. Viruses can be carried on a knife blade from plant to plant, and transfitted on the fingers of workmen.

There is no known control at the present time, and the best thing to do is to keep the plants free from all insect pests and so prevent the probable source of infection. Badly affected plants should always be burnt immediately the trouble is recognized. Weeds such as the common plantain, which can act as host plants, should always be kept down.

The greatest care should be taken to buy plants only from a reliable nurseryman. The Dahlia Growers' Association is certainly doing everything possible to try and eliminate this dreaded disease in the country. Fortunately there are certain varieties which seem to be more immune than others, and it may soon be possible to breed types and kinds which will remain free from this trouble.

The virus diseases of dahlias are so serious these days that in Holland there is a Dutch Dahlia Inspection Service. Regulations for inspection and certification have been drawn up and these have been accepted by the British authorities as a basis for the importation of Dutch dahlias. The three principal viruses with which both countries are affected are: (a) Cucumber Mosaic, (b) Spotted Wilt, and (c) Dahlia Mosaic.

One can generally recognize a virus disease by the yellowish or light-green markings on the leaves. The plants are usually dwarfed in one way or another, with the result that the flowers never look at their best. In the case of Cucumber Mosaic you usually get marks like lance-corporal stripes across the leaves, plus irregular mottling. With Spotted Wilt you can see the pale green spotting on the foliage, and often the centre of the spot will die.

With Dahlia Mosaic, the commonest of the three, there is far more stunting than with the two already mentioned. The leaf veins are banded with pale green stripes; usually only the larger veins, it is true, but with this banding one can see some wrinkling of the foliage, or a kind of mosaic pattern. Hence the name.

These virus diseases will, as I have already mentioned, attack numerous other plants in the garden. Spotted Wilt, for instance, was first discovered on tomatoes and received its name because tomatoes do wilt when attacked, although dahlia plants do not. I have seen Spotted Wilt on Arum lilies, begonias, potatoes, chrysanthemums, calceolarias and many other flowering plants. As its name suggests, Cucumber Mosaic is found on cucumbers, marrows, melons, squashes, but also, oddly enough, on delphiniums, lupins, polyanthuses and seakale spinach.

Virus 1 Dahlia Mosaic*

(Other names are Yellow Virus, Dahlia Stunt, Dwarf Virus, Dahlia Runting Virus, Dahlia Leaf-curl and Rosette Virus.)

This virus is transmissible by grafting, but is not seed-borne. The insect vector is the *Aphis myzus persicae* – sometimes called the Peach, Spinach, Potato, Brassica or Tulip aphid. It differs from the Dahlia Oakleaf virus (see below) in hosts, not being transmissible to members of the potato family.

Symptoms The normal green develops irregularly in the leaf, the areas near the veins being yellowish green and the rest of the leaf normal green. This banding varies in colour between variety and variety but is uniform within one variety. The plants show distortion or dwarfing. In some varieties leaf margins roll upwards and twist, and some varieties show shortened internodes and the subsequent forcing of lateral shoots, which in turn shorten to produce a typically 'stunted' habit. Flower stems are also short. The flowers are normal, showing no change in colour.

Control Propagate from healthy plants only. Burn diseased plants (the disease may not be very visible in some varieties). Fumigate the greenhouse to kill aphids and other insects on cuttings and seedlings.

Virus 2 Dahlia Ringspot

This is different from Tomato Spotted Wilt (see below). It is not thought to be transmissible by mechanical means, or by aphids, and the vector is at present unknown.

Symptoms Irregular concentric rings or zigzag markings, of intricate patterns. The colour of the areas varies from pale to yellowish-green, being uniform, however, within a variety. Stunting or distortion is never seen.

Virus 2A Dahlia Yellow Ringspot

This virus is treated as a variant of Virus 2.

Symptoms Bright yellow rings and zigzags. Sometimes the markings are less near the leaf tips. It differs from Virus 2 only in colour.

* I am indebted to Dr Kenneth Smith, with whom I worked years ago, for his book *Textbook of Plant Virus Diseases* published by Churchill, for much of this information.

Virus 3 Dahlia Oakleaf
Little is known.

Symptoms A pale chlorotic line across the leaf centre, very like in an oak leaf. Sometimes there are also poorly defined large yellow rings.

Virus 4 Tomato Spotted Wilt

Symptoms Clearly marked mottled rings or wavy lines on the leaves. It may be severe in seedlings, but mild on mature plants. The virus is carried from district to district in the tubers.

Control This virus is transmissible by the sap and is probably not seed transmitted. It is certainly transmitted by thrips. Therefore keep down thrips at all costs by fumigating or spraying.

17 What to do Month by Month

An author can fall into many pitfalls when he tries to give definite instructions as to what ought to be done month by month with any particular plant. What may be perfectly right for a gardener in Cornwall may be an impossibility for a keen grower at Darlington. Someone in Anglesey may be able to start his dahlias far earlier than his friend in Hull.

The directions that follow are made based largely on experience in the county of Warwickshire, where I acted as adviser for many years. This is almost in the centre of England, and so southerners will know that they may be able to get on with some work earlier, and northerners, particularly those in the north east, that they will have to wait a little longer.

It is impossible to divide the country arbitrarily into north and south. There are parts of the west that are far warmer and earlier than parts of the east. The dividing line should perhaps be between east and west, and, also, between situations sheltered from cold winds and open wind-swept situations.

January

The first New Year's resolution must be either to join the National Dahlia Society or, for readers who are already members, to make certain that the subscription for the New Year is sent to the Secretary.

Start thinking seriously about buying in new varieties for trial. In this connection write to the various specialist dahlia nurserymen for their catalogues.

Check that all the tubers in store are properly labelled, it is so easy for the writing to become obliterated. It may be necessary to rewrite with Indian ink labels that are only half decipherable.

Make quite certain that the tubers in store are not going to be ruined by frost or damp. Protect them during a freezing period by covering them up with sacking if necessary, and see that water does not drip on them.

If the weather remains open do the necessary digging and

manuring of the dahlia bed, leaving the land rough so that the frost and cold winds can act on the clods. Do not attempt to dig if there is snow on the ground.

Get everything ready for the spring: repair seed boxes, clean up old labels and repaint them with white lead paint, sharpen spades and hoes with a file, clean the blades of these tools and oil them with a 3 in 1 oil afterwards to keep them bright.

Get the 3-in. pots ready, wash and clean them so that they may be used for the first dahlia potting up in a month or two.

Buy loamless compost, which can be used for potting up the dahlias without the addition of any soil or sand.

Pot up the pot tubers, as detailed in Chapter 8.

February

Having wintered the tubers successfully, bring them into the greenhouse at the beginning of February to start them into growth.

Start to take cuttings from the dahlias the moment they appear. It will be noted that this taking of cuttings continues right the way through February and March.

As the dahlia growths start to appear keep a sharp look-out for aphids and fumigate the greenhouse with nicotine smoke.

Some gardeners will not start to take cuttings until the third week of February.

March

Continue to take cuttings. When the earlier cuttings are rooting well, pot them up into their 3-in. pots or, if you prefer, into soil blocks.

Continue to keep a sharp look-out for pests and diseases; fumigate with nicotine, using Auto-Shreds, in case of pests. If any plants show signs of virus disease scrap them immediately.

Growers who want to raise dahlias from seed should now be able to sow the seed in boxes containing John Innes Seed Compost or, better still, No-Soil Compost.

Attend carefully to whatever heating apparatus is being used for the greenhouse, for the frost must be kept out at all costs. The dahlias must be kept growing quietly but definitely.

Towards the end of the month it should be possible to get the earliest struck dahlias out into a deep frame, where they can be protected from frost and go on growing slowly.

April

There is still time to sow dahlia seed under glass.

It will be necessary to go on potting up the dahlia cuttings as they root, but it is usually neither necessary nor advisable to take any further cuttings after about the 7th of the month.

By the end of the month it should be possible, at any rate in the south, to plant out the divided tubers in accordance with the instructions given in Chapters 3 and 5.

Growers who have not ordered new dahlias, or who have not sent for any dahlia plants, should get their orders off to the nurseryman as soon as possible.

Plant out the dahlias that are going to be grown in the greenhouse for cut flowers.

May

Northerners will probably be planting out their divided dahlia tubers about 7 May in full sun.

Southerners will be planting out dahlias raised from cuttings about 20 May, when all fear of frosts should be past.

The stakes needed for the taller dahlias will be driven into the ground at the back of the plants, either before or at the time of planting.

When planting dahlias in a dry period, be sure to water thoroughly around the plants.

June

Northerners will delay the usual planting out of dahlias until about 6 June.

The soil all around the dahlias will be mulched with sedge peat 1 in. deep, which will smother the weeds and prevent the evaporation of soil moisture.

From the middle of June until about the middle of September feed fortnightly with one of the bottled liquid manures.

Stop or cut back the plants when they have produced eight pairs of leaves, to encourage the production of strong laterals.

It is not necessary to stop Dwarf Bedding Dahlias.

Towards the end of the month be prepared to reduce the number of branches to five or six, as suggested in Chapter 6.

For cut flowers provide the wire and string supports, as detailed in Chapter 7.

Make enquiries locally about horticultural shows in case you may wish to try your hand at exhibiting dahlias.

July

Start to do any necessary disbudding in order to ensure big blooms.

Keep watering the dahlia beds if the weather is very dry. The water can always be given through the sedge peat, if this has been applied.

Attend to the staking and tying-up of the taller dahlias.

Keep picking off the dead dahlia flowers from now until the end of October if necessary.

Watch out for pests and diseases and control them with the insecticides and fungicides mentioned in Chapter 15.

August

Continue with necessary disbudding.

Hoe the ground lightly, using a Dutch hoe if the sedge peat mulching method has been adopted.

Watch out for pests and diseases and apply the necessary remedies as detailed in Chapter 15.

Particular care must be taken this month in respect of earwigs and ants.

Feed regularly with liquid manure if this is necessary.

September

Keep on picking off the dead heads of the dahlias, especially in the case of bedding varieties.

There may easily be a frost by about 23 September in the north, so be prepared to protect the plants in some way if it is desired to keep them flowering longer.

Continue to feed the plants once a fortnight with one of the liquid manures.

Attend to the tying up, if this is necessary.

Keep on disbudding if bigger blooms are needed.

Look over the plants carefully and, if there are any signs of virus, scrap the infected specimens immediately and burn them.

Try and attend any dahlia shows there may be, in order to learn more about dahlias.

This is a good month to go round dahlia nurseries and look at the varieties growing *in situ*. Aim to do this, however, during the first ten days of the month.

October

When the dahlias have been cut down to the ground by frost, leave them in the soil for about ten days and then dig up the tubers ready to be brought indoors under cover.

The frozen tops may be cut down to within 4 in. of soil level and be put on to the compost heap.

Store the dahlias carefully in a frost-proof room or shed where the tubers will not shrivel because it is too dry or rot because it is too wet.

Remember that it is possible to store the roots in trenches. For details of this see the last three paragraphs of Chapter 3.

Enquire from a dahlia nurseryman whether he would be prepared to sell you tubers of the varieties you hope to grow next year. You can thus propagate your own next February or March.

November

Keep a sharp look-out for trouble with the tubers in store, remembering that they may be surrounded by dry sedge peat to prevent them from drying out; this peat must not get sodden. The tubers must never be touched by frost.

Aim to look at your tubers every ten days or so. There may be trouble with rats or mice, or even with a leaky roof.

It is possible to buy in tubers from the nurseryman rather than buy plants, and these can be stored in a similar way to your own.

December

Continue to take the utmost care of your dahlias in store, bearing in mind the remarks made in November.

Spend your winter evenings reading the handbook of the National Dahlia Society and studying the classified list of dahlias.

Give your friends a copy of *The Basic Book of Dahlia Growing*, to encourage them to start dahlia growing!

Encourage your friends to join the National Dahlia Society.

Appendix

There is a tremendous amount of odd information which will be of use to keen growers of dahlias. Readers who feel that further information is needed on other subjects connected with dahlias should kindly write to me. I am most anxious to make this dahlia book as complete as possible, and in the past readers have been tremendously kind in making suggestions.

Sizes of Flower Pots

Flower pots are made in definite sizes and the name given to them refers to the number of pots of that particular size that could be made out of the normal 'caste' of clay. Now that flower pots are made of plastic the original sizes and measurements have very often been followed. Thus the 'sixty', which is a clay pot measuring 3 in diameter at the top and 3½ in in depth is still called a 'sixty', even though it may be made of some plastic material.

FLOWER POT SIZES

Term Used	*Diameter at top of Pot*	*Depth of Pot*
	in.	in.
Sixties (60s)	3	3½
Forty-eights (48s)	4½	5
Thirty-twos (32s)	6	6
Twenty-fours (24s)	8½	8
Sixteens (16s)	9½	9

The Seasons

Spring commences 21 March, lasts 92 days 21 hours
Summer commences 21 June, lasts 93 days 14 hours
Autumn commences 23 September, lasts 89 days 17¾ hours
Winter commences 21 December, lasts 89 days 1 hour

Fimbriated Dahlias

The nursery firm called Keynes Williams introduced a new dahlia, in the year 1900, called 'Progenitor' whose florets were said to be furcated. Since 1900 many different furcated Cactus Dahlia varieties have been introduced. So in 1959 the National Dahlia Society introduced into their show schedule a class for Fimbriated or Furcated Dahlias.

Quite a large number of varieties are now being raised on the Continent, while in this country Mr H. Stredwick, VMH, has raised a number of first-class varieties. In the United States of America they have also introduced a number of new kinds; there they described as Stagshorn or Forked Dahlias.

It is understood that the Joint Dahlia Committee of the National Dahlia Society and the Royal Horticultural Society is to consider introducing a separate classification for Furcated or Fimbriated Cactus Dahlias, and if this is done, then it is probable that the word Fimbriated will be adopted as the name and the other descriptions (Furcated, Stagshorn and Forked) dropped completely. If you are hoping to exhibit, note whether the show schedule gives details of Fimbriated Dahlias. If they are mentioned you may like to try three varieties: 'Dentelle de Venise', 'Folies de Dentelle' and 'Popular Guest'.

Gardeners who are sensible enough to join the National Dahlia Society will, of course, be receiving an official notification in the Dahlia Yearbook when the special classification for Fimbriated Cactus Dahlias is adopted. This will give them plenty of time to make their entries in the shows, while in addition show committees will know early enough to enable them to alter their schedules if they consider this advisable and necessary.

Lime and Soil Acidity

Soil containing less than one part of lime in two hundred parts of soil cannot be brought into a high state of fertility. Lime can help to correct undesirable soil conditions and may therefore be regarded as a soil improving agent. It also provides the calcium needed as a food by the dahlias. It improves the texture of heavy soils by making them more pliable and workable.

Lime counteracts the acidity in the soil and so enables the micro-organisms to work in an unrestricted manner. (Their activities are daily associated with fertility.) Lime ensures the right decomposition of organic matter and renders the soil phosphates more available. It has a neutralizing affect on the acids of peaty soils and in sandy soils it helps to release potash.

Scientists have agreed to express the degree of acidity in the soil by what may seem a strange notation: pH7 represents the neutral point. Figures less than 7 indicate a degree of acidity and figures more than 7 indicate a degree of alkalinity. pH4, for instance is a much more acid soil than pH6.

The dahlia grower in Great Britain is likely to find that the extremes run between pH8.5 and pH4.5, and it is thought that dahlias do best on soils which range from pH6 to pH7.5. Now to find out the soil's pH it is necessary to use indicating fluid. This is green in colour and when it comes in contact with the soil it will turn to orange, red, or yellow; the colour will show the gardener exactly the degree of acidity or alkalinity present. A chart is supplied with the fluid, and he can compare the colour of the fluid after it has been in contact with the soil with the corresponding colour on the chart; from this he knows the exact pH.

A number of firms, including British Drug Houses, produce soil indicating fluid. It may be bought from any good retail chemist.

To raise the pH from pH4 to pH7 would require, with sandy soil, about 4 tons of lime per acre. But if you happen to have a garden where the soil is a very heavy clay you would have to use lime at the rate of 12 tons per acre, i.e. three times as much. If you discover that your soil is pH6 and you want to raise it to pH7, you would only need $1\frac{1}{2}$ tons per acre with sandy soil but 3 tons per acre with clay soil.

A dressing of 1 ton per acre means giving $7\frac{1}{2}$oz per square yard, and, of course, for 2 tons per acre it will be 15 oz per square yard.

There is always a certain loss of lime each year. In the West Country, where the rainfall is heavy, the annual loss of lime per acre in the drainage water may be as much as 6 cwt per acre. In addition, of course, the dahlias themselves remove a certain amount of lime each year, probably about 1 cwt per acre. It is therefore necessary to consider lime and acidity. If, however, dahlias are planted in different parts of the garden each year, in some form of rotation, there is always the possibility that the previous crop was well limed and so there will not be the same need to give special dressings of lime for the dahlias.

Limes are usually compared on the basis of their calcium oxide content. The pH indicator always refers to the amount of quick lime to be used. If the soil test indicates that 1 ton of quick lime is required, the alternative would be to use $1\frac{1}{4}$ tons of hydrated lime, or $1\frac{3}{4}$ tons of ground limestone. I prefer ground limestone every time because it does not burn like quick lime or ground lime, and is much easier to spread than hydrated lime.

Furthermore, ground limestone or carbonate of lime is easy to store.

The diagram below will show clearly what is meant by the pH scale.

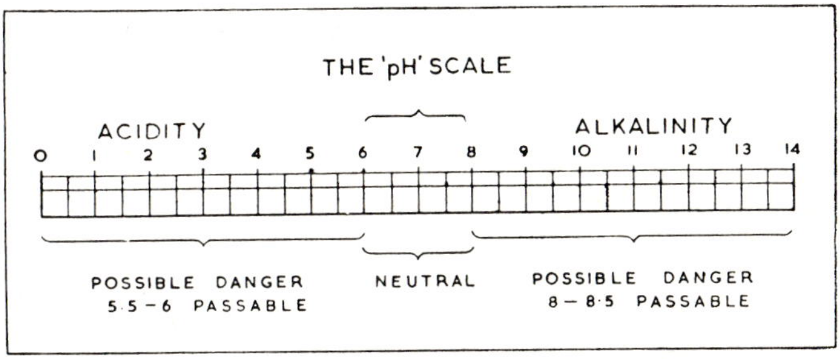

The following notes will serve to underline a few points, and also to clarify some further matters.

1. Never mix lime with farmyard manure or dung.

2. Remember that lime improves the soil texture of heavy clays.

3. Lime is a plant food and provides calcium.

4. Lime keeps the soil 'sweet' and prevents acidity.

5. Chalk or limestone is ground and sold as ground limestone.

6. Quick lime, lump lime or Buxton lime is in fact oxide of lime.

7. Hydrated lime is slaked oxide of lime.

8. Ground quick lime is sold as ground lime.

9. Note the difference between ground limestone and ground lime.

10. If directed to use ground lime at 3 oz to the square yard you would have to use ground limestone at 7 oz per square yard or hydrated lime at 5 oz to the square yard. Please note the comparison between the three.

11. Growers who want accurate figures in respect of lime application should always use soil indicating fluid. This is green and may be bought in a bottle from a retail chemist.

12. Lime should always be applied to the surface of the soil after the preparation of the land is complete, and should never be forked in. Always let the rain wash it in.

Liquid Feeding

In the old days liquid manures were obtained by putting a sack of cow manure or sheep manure into a tub of rainwater and leaving it there for a month or so. The liquid thus produced was used for feeding plants. These liquid manures might easily contain diseases, and so today most keen dahlia growers prefer to buy liquid manures in bottles or cans. The manures are made up to a definite formula, and diluted in accordance with the instructions on the labels. They will be used for feeding plants regularly, and they are also of great value on compost heaps.

Some of these liquid manures are made entirely from organic matter, such as seaweed; others are prepared from urine, certain other plant foods being added later to balance them up.

It is surprising what small doses of liquid manure will prove effective. The homeopath would of course understand the reasons for this. If, for instance, a teaspoonful (which is equal to $\frac{1}{8}$oz) of one of the bottled liquid manures is placed in a gallon of water (160oz), and the two are mixed together, there will be roughly 125 parts of nitrogen, 110 parts of phosphoric acid and 55 parts of potassium per 1 million parts of water. This appears to be a very small dose indeed, but it is better than the normal nutrient concentration found in the soil solution of any well-manured dahlia bed. The great advantage of using liquid food is that the food reaches the root hairs without having to undergo any further dilution and so can be taken up by the plants immediately.

I am sometimes asked to give definite advice as to the quantities of liquid manure that should be used. For dahlias 1 gallon should be sufficient for a 6ft row when the plants are about a quarter grown; this could be doubled when the plants are half grown. It is impossible to be precise as to when these liquid manures should be used, but generally speaking successful gardeners aim to feed about once a fortnight during the main growing season. Experts, however, prefer to give liquid feeds only when they feel that the plants need help, and so only they can decide when this should be done.

Raising New Varieties

With the definite exception of Coltness Hybrid Dahlias, very few dahlias come true from seed. Growers who try and raise new varieties must realize that only one seedling in 1,000 is found to be better than its parents. Dahlia blooms consist of (a) ray florets and (b) disc florets. The disc florets contain both male and female organs, while the ray florets usually contain female organs but hardly ever male organs. It is the male organs or stamens that produce the pollen. Pollen must be dropped or placed on to the surface of the female organs, or stigmas, so that fertilization may take place and the seed be formed.

Now, with single flowers there is usually plenty of male pollen, but with double dahlias it is extremely difficult to discover disc florets in which there are males and suitable pollen. It is true that males are sometimes discovered within certain central disc florets when a bloom has almost withered. Most natural pollination is done by bees and other visiting insects, and some nurserymen rely on these chance 'crossings'. All they have to do is to collect any fully developed pods in the autumn.

If, on the other hand, a gardener desires to try his hand at some definite 'mating', then he must transfer the pollen himself, using a small camel's-hair brush, from one flower to another. To prevent the possibility of the bloom being visited by some insect it is necessary to cover the dahlia flower to be pollinated with a suitable muslin bag both before and after pollination. It is also necessary to remove the disc florets which may contain the male organs. The result of this careful hand pollination should be the production of a seed pod with numerous seeds in it, the definite beginnings of a new variety.

The great trouble about trying to do this work in Britain is that we usually have such appalling weather in the autumn, and often the seed pods rot away long before the seed has a chance of ripening and maturing. It is much easier to carry out the work in South Africa, Australia and New Zealand. Naturally, if one aims to produce a first-class new variety, it is essential to take care over choosing the parentage. Unfortunately there are good varieties which are known to give poor results, and therefore the beginner must be satisfied in making his experiments over a number of years. After, say, ten years of disappointments he may suddenly find that he has produced a superb variety.

Because this artificial transference of pollen from one flower to another on a camel's-hair brush isn't particularly easy, another method often adopted is to plant close together the varieties that are to be crossed. By keeping bees or allowing a local beekeeper to put a hive in his garden, the dahlia grower hopes that the bees will do the necessary work for him. When seed pods have resulted he collects the seeds and sows them in due course.

Fortunately with dahlias one can get a full-size flowering

plant within the first year; one does not have to wait ten years or more as in the case of apples. The seedlings should be planted out as close as 9 in apart, so that they take up very little room in the garden, and at the end of the first season it must be decided which of the seedlings should be kept for another year. One certainly has to be very hard-hearted at this time; to a beginner's eye all the 'ducks' may appear to be 'swans'.

Sports

Sometimes the beginner to dahlia growing discovers with astonishment that one plant in his garden, of a variety that should bear yellow blooms, has one one side of it a branch bearing, say, pink flowers of a similar size and shape. If these variations are not produced as the result of pollination and fertilization, but by vegetative propagation, they are called 'sports'. Officially they may be referred to as mutations. Changes take place in the cell make-up of one branch of the plant which may result either in some part of the bloom being affected or, as has already been said, the whole bloom. No one exactly knows how these sports take place, or why. The fact is that they do, and they can be perpetuated by the taking of cuttings. Please, therefore, note any sports that may occur in your own garden and either take the trouble to perpetuate them yourself or offer them to some local nurseryman.

Non-tubering

Sometimes dahlias will produce no tubers at all. This has nothing to do with the British weather: I have come across this trouble in many different parts of the world. When the plants are cut down at the end of their flowering season, and dug up, thick roots are found instead of the normal tuber formation. This, of course, makes the grower very worried because now he has no means of propagating his stock.

The trouble is due to a number of reasons. In the first place, the raising of new varieties has generally been done, naturally, with an eye to the size and colour of the bloom, the brightness of the foliage, and the strength of the stem. Few raisers have bothered at all about producing new varieties that will grow good tubers. It has been suggested that this is because nurserymen do not want amateurs to be in a position to raise their own plants, and expect them to buy new stock each year. But this cannot be true, because if the variety is normally non-tuberous then the nurseryman himself will meet with similar problems of cutting production.

It is to be hoped that for the sake of the good name of the dahlia more attention will be paid to tubers in the future. There are varieties at the moment which are very disappointing, not because they do not produce good flowers but because they do not propagate successfully year after year.

There is a more obvious cause for poor tuber production, and that is late planting. The dahlia must be given a chance of building up its tubers over a long period. Then, again, land that is low in humus content makes for poor tubers. Sandy soils, especially in the dryer parts of the world, often give poor results in this connection.

When it is found that a particular variety does not produce sufficient tubers it is advisable to save the old roots and either propagate them by division or, if they are large enough, plant them out the following season as they are. I have discovered that if old roots are planted again the following season, tubers may be built up the following year, and it is from these that cuttings will be produced. Another way of trying to force a plant to produce tubers is to pot up a few of the plants into 3 in pots and keep them growing in these the whole of the season. Because the roots are restricted and because comparatively little growth can be made above, the tubers formed in the pots will be small. These are usually called pot-tubers by dahlia growers. From these pot-tubers cuttings can usually be produced without any difficulty. There is no need, by the way, to keep the pots out of the ground; early in June they may be plunged into the soil up to their rims, which will reduce watering to a minimum.

The Problem of Hollow Cuttings

Beginners sometimes complain that the first few shoots that grow out from the junction of an old stem and a tuber are thick and hollow. They find that these hollow cuttings do not strike as they should, refusing to grow roots. Actually, in my experience, they do root eventually but they take a very long time. Because these early cuttings do not root quickly the beginner makes up his mind that in future he will take his cuttings with a tiny portion of the old tuber attached at the base. Having done this, he discovers that he gets excellent results, for such cuttings taken with a heel root very quickly indeed and produce excellent plants.

The great trouble with preparing and making cuttings in this way is that you get far fewer cuttings because you remove the bud or eye from which the young shoots are produced. It is always better, therefore, to cut the earlier produced shoots, even if they are hollow, with a razor blade or a sharp knife at a point $\frac{1}{4}$in above the tuber. (The hollow cuttings may have to be discarded.) This, of course, leaves the base of the hollow shoot on the old tuber and the hard pruning back, as one may call it, stimulates the dormant buds below, with the result that these start growing, producing thinner shoots that will make good cuttings and strike readily. I find it best to take such cuttings when they are about 3 in long and to remove them (again, with a sharp knife) just below the first pair of leaves.

Special Service to Members of the National Dahlia Society

Any member of the National Dahlia Society may, if they wish, submit blooms to the Classification Committee for classification as to section, class and colour group.

The Committee requires not less than six open blooms of a variety with flowers less than 6in in diameter, and not fewer than three blooms of any other variety.

Forms may be obtained from the General Secretary of the National Dahlia Society (Mr Philip Damp, 26 Burns Road, Leamington Spa, Warwickshire). The Secretary will advise applicants of the time and place of the next meeting, and blooms should be forwarded or brought to the venue in time to reach the Hon. Secretary of the Classification Committee at least one hour before the beginning of this meeting.

No charge is made for this service, but a stamped addressed envelope should be forwarded when a reply is required.

More Notes on the Classification of Dahlias

A few not normally classified, but grown quite widely, may be mentioned here:

DWARF BEDDING

Unwins Dwarf Hybrids: generally grown from seed, not offered in named varieties, mixed range of colours.

Unwins Advance: a superior type of the above, with brilliant colours; mostly semi-double and fully double flowers.

DWARF MINIATURE SINGLE BEDDING

Lilliput (approx. $1\frac{1}{2}$–2ft): single flowers, approx. 2in. in diameter.

Topmix (approx. 12in): in a wide colour range, sold as separate colours (plants or tubers). The smallest single dahlia, flowers 1–2in in diameter. Useful for small arrangements of flowers, and for front row bedding.

Dahlia Trials

Experiments carried out at the Lee Valley Horticultural Research Station with dahlias, some raised from tubers and others propagated from cuttings, have shown a higher yield of blooms per plant, in the early stages, from tubers.

Tubers were planted between 27 April and 29 April, and the cuttings on 30 and 31 May, spacing for both being 2ft square and manuring being John Innes Base Fertilizer at 8oz per square yard.

Cutting from the plants grown from tubers began on 1 July, and from cutting-grown plants on 4 July. By 19 July, the average numbers of blooms produced from certain varieties were as follows (figures for cutting-grown plants in brackets): Edinburgh 17 (3.4); Brilliant 8.7 (3.1); Shirley Westwell 7.3 (4.6); Jean Lister 1.6 (5.6).

R. H. Gardner, Director, pointed out that the outdoor planting of tubers can be undertaken much earlier than with rooted cuttings, since spring frosts will not destroy tubers.

Index

Abbreviations 15
Access Frames 41, 56
'Alex No-Soil' composts 37
Anemone flowered 13, 16, 130
Ants 139, 140
Aphids 134, 137, 139, 140, 149
Azo Benzene fumigants 144

Ball 16, 18, 83, 127–8, 114
Bedding out 92
Beds and bedding 76, 94
–designs 91–2
–edges 93
–plants 91–7
–preparation and maintenance 93–5
–variety of dahlia 59, 70, 91–2, 95, 166
Beetle 134
Beyond the Microscope 149
'Bio Plant Food' 88
Bishop of Llandaff 83, 92, 131
Black spot 135
Blue striped wilt 148
Bone meal 52
Bordeaux mixture 138
Botrytis 31
'Bouisol' 148
Bouquet 13
Bran and Paris green 139
Burgundy mixture 138
Bute, Marchioness of 11

Cactus-flowered 13, 17, 59, 70, 73, 82, 109–13, 114, 148
–giant 111
–incurved 110
–medium 112
–miniature 35
–straight 110
Capsid bugs 139, 140
'Captan' 138, 148
Carbonate of lime 46
Catalogues 153
Caterpillars 76, 100, 134, 137, 139, 141
Charms 59, 76
Chlorosis, lime-induced 46
Chrysanthemums 68
Classification 15–20, 166
Classified List of Dahlias and Guide for Judges, The 108
Cloches 56
Coccinea 12, 13
Cold frames 41
Collarettes 16, 59, 129–30
Colloidal copper 139
Colloidal sulphur 139
Colour classification 18–20
Coltness Gem 14, 91
Coltness Hybrid 162
Commercial growing 78
Compost 36, 44, 65
–John Innes 21, 23
–No-Soil 37
Compost heap 50
Crimson Flag 77
Crown Call 147
Crutch bloom 69
Cuckoo Spit 141
Cucumber mosaic 150
Cultivars 18
Cut flowers 77–83
–best types 77, 81
–lasting time 77
Cutting back 68–70
Cuttings 28–42
–boxes 38
–dibbling in 37, 38
–hardening off 40–2, 57
–hollow 165
–labelling 33, 36
–planting out 40
–potting on 42
–preparing and striking 34–6, 40, 57
–propagation frame 33
–rooting 32, 35, 36, 38
–watering 36
–when to take 32
Cutworms 134, 142

Dahl, Dr. A. 11
Dahlia mosaic 150, 151
Dahlia oakleaf 152
Dahlia ringspot 151
Dahlia yellow ringspot 151
decoratives 16, 59, 81, 114–24
–giant 87, 115
–large 34, 71, 73, 87, 118
–medium 59, 73, 118
–miniature 81, 123
–small 59, 81, 121
Denitrification 48
Derris dust 138
Disbudding 59, 75–6
Diseases and pests 21, 22, 47, 90, 134–52
Dis-shooting 86
'Dowpon' 54
Drainage 135
'Draza' 144
Dried blood 52
Dry rot 148
Dry season 84
Dust Guns 137
Dutch hoe 65, 135
Dutch Light 38, 88–9
Dwarf 70, 91, 95

Earthworms 46, 47
Earwigs 76, 100, 134, 140, 141, 142
Exhibitions 13, 57, 60, 98–108
–growing for 98–100
–varieties 101
Expense 24

Farmyard manure 47–8
Feeding 67–8, 87–9, 95
Fermentation 31
Fertilizer 22, 47, 51–3, 78
Fimbriated 158–9
Fish manure 49, 50, 53, 68, 78
Flue dust 52
Frames 41–2
Frost 28, 31, 56
–protection against 63
Frustanea 12
Fumigation 90, 137, 139, 144
Fungicides 138
Fungus diseases 31, 90, 134–6, 147–9

'Gammexane' 146
Gardener's Dictionary, The
Geranium 91
Golden Heart 34
Grafting 27–8
Grass 93
Green manure 49
Greenfly *see Aphids*
Greenhouses
–best type 90
–border 89
–growing in 84–90
–heating 27, 28, 33, 42, 86
–staging 38
Grocinea 13
Guano 53

Height 60
History 11–14
(*see also chapters on specific types*)
Hoof and horn meal 52
Hops 48
Hormones 37
Hornets 146
Humus 47

Icones 13
Insecticides 90, 137–8, 139
Insects 134

'John Innes' composts 21, 23
Juarezii 13, 109

'Karathane' 138

Leaf miners 139
Leather jackets 139
Lilliputian 13
Lime 45–6, 159
Lime-induced chlorosis 46
Liquid derris 137
Liquid food 88, 162
'Bio Plant Food' 88 –
Liver of sulphur 138

Manure and manuring 53–4, 135
–liquid 54, 68, 78, 162
Meat and bone meal 53
Metaldehyde 144
Mildew 31, 135, 138
Mohair 20
Month by month timetable 153–7
Mulching 25, 49, 65–6, 78

National Dahlia Society 13, 15, 153, 166
Nicotine 137, 140, 145
'Nippon' 139, 140
Nitrogen 52
Non-tubering 149, 164

Orchid-flowering 18, 130

Paeony-flowering 16, 59, 114, 131
Peat, sedge 32, 49
Pests *see Diseases and pests*
Peter Ramsey 34
pH indicator 46, 160
Philips lamps 84
Phosphates 62
Pinnata 13
Planting 56–64
–distances 59–61
–nursery plants 62
–planning 60–1
–situation 58
–when to 56, 78–9
–zig-zag method 60
Planting out 94
–when to 78–9
Pollination 24, 163
Pompons 13, 17, 18, 59, 77, 81, 83, 90, 99, 103, 125–6, 148
Potash 52, 68
Pots 40
–Jiffy 40
–six inch 86
–sizes 158
Propagation 11, 21–43
–hormones 37
–seed sowing 21–5
Protection 73–4, 99

Red spiders 134, 137, 139, 143
Rosea 12, 13
Rotary cultivator 78
Rothesay Superb 34
Rotting 31
Royal Encyclopaedia 11
Rust 135
Rye grass 50

Salvia 91
Sand 32
Sawdust 65
Seasons 158
Seaweed 48
Seeds
–merchants 21
–new varieties 24
–pricking off 23
–sowing 22
–temperature 23
–watering 22
Semi-cactus 17, 73, 82, 109–13
–giant 111
–large-flowered 112
–medium-flowered 112
Sewage 48
Shade and shading 58, 77, 99
Shoddy 48
Single flowered 13, 16, 131–2
'Slugit' 144
Slugs and snails 134, 144
Smut 135, 147
Soil
–acidity 45, 159
–blocks 39
–drainage 46
–dry 57
–preparing and feeding 44–55
–sodden 57
–sterilization 147
–types 44–5, 46, 61, 74
Soil indicator fluid 46
Solo sprayers 136
Soot 52
Sports 164
Spotted wilt 150
Sprayers and dusters 136–7
Staking and supporting 62, 70–3, 88
–bamboo canes 70, 71, 100
–galvanised stakes 71
–peasticks 73
–posts 79
–tying 71–2
–wires 79
Stars 59, 132
Steamed bone flour 52
Stem thinning 73–5
Stopping 68–70
Straw 65, 78
Sun 58
Superflua 12

Tares 50
Thrips 139, 145, 149
Timing *see Stopping*
Tomato spotted wilt 152
'Topmix' 132–3, 167
Trials 167
Tubers 12
–cutting back 33
–digging up 28
–division 25–7
–frost damage 28
–labelling 28, 43
–planting out 58, 64, 89
–potting up, 85–6
–pruning 33
–storage 29–31, 43, 85, 148
Twiggy 80

Variabilis 12
Varieties 81–3, 95
–new 162–4
Vectors 134, 151

'Vermiculite' 39
Virus diseases 149–52

Wasps 145
Watering 62–4, 66–7, 78, 94
Weed killers 50
–Dowpon 54–5
–hormone 54–5
–SBK 54
Weeds and weeding 54, 65, 136
White fly 139
Wilt 148
Wind damage 63, 77
Wire worms 134, 146
Wood ashes 52, 68
Woodlice 146